WASHINGTON

WASHINGTON BY ROAD

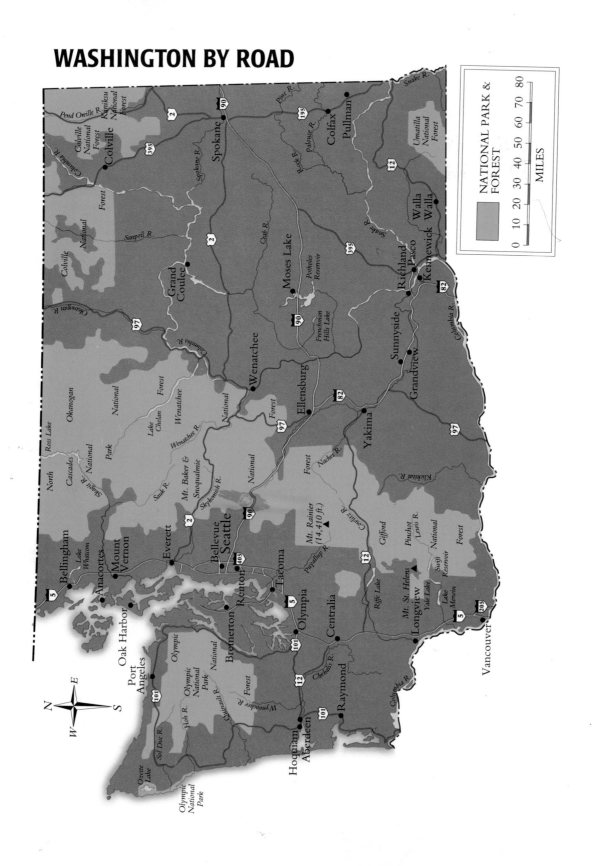

NATIONAL PARK & FOREST

MILES

0 10 20 30 40 50 60 70 80

CELEBRATE THE STATES
WASHINGTON

Rebecca Stefoff

BENCHMARK BOOKS

MARSHALL CAVENDISH
NEW YORK

Benchmark Books
Marshall Cavendish Corporation
99 White Plains Road
Tarrytown, New York 10591-9001

Library of Congress Cataloging-in-Publication Data
Stefoff, Rebecca
Washington / Rebecca Stefoff.
p.   cm. — (Celebrate the States)
Includes bibliographical references and index.
Summary: An introduction to the geography, history, government,
economy, people, achievements, and landmarks of the Evergreen State.
ISBN 0-7614-0422-8 (lib. bdg.)
1. Washington (State)—Juvenile literature. [1. Washington (State)] I. Title. II. Series.
F891.3.S72   1999   917.97—dc21   97-48937   CIP   AC

Maps and graphics supplied by Oxford Cartographers, Oxford, England

Photo research by Ellen Barrett Dudley and Matthew Joseph Dudley

Cover photo: Photo Researchers, Inc. / Michael P. Gadomski

The photographs in this book are used by permission and through the courtesy of: *Photo Reserachers, Inc.*:
Jim Steinberg, 6-7; Pat & Tom Leeson, 13, 61, 112; Jim Corwin, 15, 104; Porterfield/Chickering, 25; Stephen
J. Krasemann, 26, 118(top); Alain Thomas, 51; David R. Frazier, 65; Ken Cavanaugh, 66; Chromosohn/Sohm,
77; F. Stuart Westmorland, 80, 98-99, 108; John M. Burnley, 109; Leonard Lee Rue, 115(top); Kaj R.
Svensson/Library Science Photo, 115(bottom); Renee Lynn, 118(bottom). *Renee DeMartin*: 10-11, 23(bottom),
28, 59, 105. *The Image Bank*: D. William Hamilton, 17; Chuck Kuhn, 63, 72; Anthony Boccaccio, 64, 107;
Steve Satushek, back cover. *Borland Stock Photo*: Charlie Borland, 20, 81. *Affordable Photo Stock*: Francis/Donna
Caldwell, 23(top), 68-69, 74, 78, 111, 132; Francis E. Caldwell, 86-87, 123. *Frye Art Museum, Seattle,
Washington*: 30-31. *Royal Ontario Museum*: 33. *Washington State Historical Society, Tacoma, Washington*: 35, 48,
49. *Denver Public Library, Western History Department*: 37, 39. *#10157(a) D. Kinsey Collection, Whatcom
Museum of History and Art, Bellingham, WA*: 42. *Tacoma Public Library, Northwestern Room*: 44. *C/Z Harris*:
52-53. *The Seattle Times*: 56. *Calvin Larson*: 60, 121. *Greater Poulsbo Chamber of Commerce*: 73. *Dale Chihuly,
Honolulu Academy of Arts, 1992 Photo: Russel Johnson*: 82. *Washington State Tourism Division*: 84. *Corbis-
Bettmann*: 89. *The Artist and the Francine Seders Gallery, Seattle, WA/ Photo by Spike Mafford*: 90. *Archive Photos*:
91, 94, 129(bottom); Reuters/Kamal Kishore, 92; Reuters/Blake Sell, 96; American Stock, 126; Ron Sachs
Consolidated News Pictures, 127(top); Peter Turnley/New York Times Co., 129(top). *James Chatters*: 95.
State of Washington, Secretary of States Office: 114(bottom). *The Boeing Company Corporate Identity*: 125(top).
Corbis-Bettmann/UPI: 125(bottom), 127(bottom).

Printed in Italy

1   3   5   6   4   2

CONTENTS

WASHINGTON IS . . . .

Washington is layer upon layer of history.

"Every part of this country is sacred to my people. Every hillside, every valley, every plain and grove has been hallowed by some fond memory or some sad experience of my tribe."

—Chief Seattle, 1854

"I remember it rained awful hard that day . . . and the last glimpse I had of them was the women standing under the trees with their wet bonnets over their faces and their aprons to their eyes."

—Description of pioneer families arriving in 1851

"For the first time I met Seattle face to face. It was a far cry from the splendid city of today. . . . [But] the blue waters, lush evergreens, and snow-capped mountain ranges on the horizon were to a great extent the font of what inhabitants hail as the Seattle spirit."

—Nellie Cornish, who came to Washington in 1900

Its people have big plans for the future.

"The Pacific age is coming, and the Northwest is right on the edge of it. I'm studying Chinese—everything's going to be happening between here and China."   —Fifteen-year-old Dave Rickhart

"A new century is coming at us like a bullet train. And it's up to us to either rise to challenges or watch as that train passes by."

—Governor Gary Locke, 1997

The state has attracted many newcomers in recent years . . .

"You wonder why I love it here? This whole state is beautiful! When we came here on vacation I knew I wanted to spend the rest of my life here. There's boating and skiing and hiking, and a fabulous world-class city. Look at those mountains! The rain? Well, if you're lucky you can get away from it for a week in Mexico or Hawaii."

—Darren Peralta, who moved from Massachusetts
to the Olympic Peninsula

. . . but not everyone is thrilled by the area's popularity.

"The first place that Californians ruined was southern Oregon. Twenty years later they moved here and helped ruin this place."

—Longtime Whidbey Island resident, 1995

"Tell your readers it rains all the time. Tell 'em we have horrible crime. Tell 'em to visit all they want but not to move here."

—Puget Sound resident to magazine writer

From green hills lapped by the blue Pacific to golden-brown interior plains, Washington is a state of contradictions. Rain forest and sunbaked outback. Big city and small town. Logger and environmentalist. Urban trendsetter and range-riding cowboy. Blessed—or cursed—with a reputation as one of America's best places to live, Washington draws people from around the world. Newcomers and old-timers alike have visions of what the state should be. Their challenge is to find a vision that all can share.

1 SOME OF EVERYTHING

"I wanted to take a boat trip on the ocean," says twelve-year-old Kelleen Houk from Maryland, explaining why her family chose Washington for their summer vacation. "My little brother wanted to see a cowboy ranch. And my big brother wanted to climb a mountain. My mom found out that Washington has all that stuff."

As the Houks discovered, Washington has plenty of variety—and enough natural beauty for a dozen states. Washington is one of the Pacific Northwest states. The Pacific Ocean borders it on the west. On the south is Oregon, on the east is Idaho, and on the north is British Columbia, part of Canada. Within Washington's borders are towering mountains, rushing rivers, sunbaked prairies, dense forests, and craggy fields of dry, broken lava.

LAND AND REGIONS

Washington owes its varied geography to the chain of mountains that runs through it, splitting it into two parts, the east side and the west side. Those mountains are the Cascades, the state's backbone. The tallest peak is Mount Rainier, at 14,410 feet. On clear days Rainier's broad-shouldered, white-topped dome can be seen from many miles away, glowing pink or gold at sunrise or sunset.

The Cascades are volcanoes, and they are still alive. Beneath their surface, lava bubbles and steam hisses. One of Washington's

People watched the violent 1980 explosion of Mount St. Helens from many miles away. Closer to the volcano, churning rivers of hot mud buried 150 square miles of countryside.

volcanoes erupted on May 18, 1980. Mount St. Helens blew its top, sending a vast cloud of ash and steam high into the air. Rivers of hot mud poured down the mountainside, ripping trees from the ground and clogging rivers. About sixty people died, and a thick layer of ash fell like gray snow over hundreds of square miles. The ash cloud created such darkness that people as far away as Yakima, in central Washington, had to drive with their headlights on in midday.

Northeastern Washington, called the Okanogan Highlands, is covered with low, rugged mountains that spread into Canada and Idaho. South of the highlands is the Columbia Plateau, a high, dry prairie that covers much of east-central Washington. The plateau is a giant lava bed—one of the largest and thickest in the world. Thousands of years ago volcanoes spilled layer after layer of lava across the land. Later, enormous floods rushed across it, carving deep, narrow trenches called coulees. Along Washington's southeastern border is the Palouse, a region of gently rolling, rounded hills covered with a thick, fertile layer of windblown soil. The wheat fields of the Palouse throw a quilt of vivid colors over the land.

Washington's largest river, the Columbia, flows south from Canada, sweeping through central Washington in a huge loop before it flows west into the Pacific. The lower Columbia marks the border with Oregon. Once the Columbia was one of America's mightiest rivers, a rushing torrent with many waterfalls and rapids. Dams have slowed its flow and turned it into a string of sluggish lakes. The dams provide water to irrigate the plateau and the Palouse. They also produce hydroelectric power for industries and homes throughout the Pacific Northwest.

If you climbed a high peak in the Cascades and looked down at the western third of Washington, you would see a patchwork of green and blue, a mixture of land and water. The Skykomish, Skagit, Snoqualmie, and dozens of other rivers tumble down the mountain slopes to the Puget Sound Lowland, a flat strip of land sandwiched between the Cascades and the jumbled geography of the state's western edge. Nearly three-quarters of Washington's people live in the Puget Sound Lowland.

In the north, the lowland curves around Puget Sound, a long, deep arm of the Pacific that cuts into the heart of Washington. Centuries ago huge ice sheets called glaciers crawled over this land, carving channels into it. When the ice retreated, the sea flowed into the channels and created the maze of waterways that is the sound. Hundreds of islands dot its surface. Some are merely craggy boulders

"The lion-colored land" is how Washington poet Marie Ledbetter describes the Palouse region.

A LEGEND CROSSES THE COLUMBIA

A thousand years ago a huge landslide blocked the Columbia River. Over time the river washed out the base of this "dam," leaving a natural bridge of earth and rock connecting the two banks.

The Chinook Indians called this bridge the Great Cross Over and said that the Great Spirit had placed two of his sons, in the form of mountains, on either side of the bridge—Klickitat on the north and Wyeast on the south. All went well until beautiful Squaw Mountain moved into the neighborhood. Although she loved Wyeast, she liked to flirt with Klickitat. Soon the brothers were fighting over her, stamping and spitting fire and ash into the air and hurling rocks across the river at one another. Their rumblings shook the Great Cross Over so hard that it crumbled into the river.

Klickitat was bigger than Wyeast, and he won the battle. Wyeast gave up Squaw Mountain, who sadly took her place at Klickitat's side. But because she still loved Wyeast, she went to sleep and never woke up. To this day Klickitat stands over her with bowed head.

The mountains that the Indians called sons of the Great Spirit are volcanoes in the Cascades. Wyeast is Oregon's Mt. Hood. Klickitat is Washington's Mt. Adams. Squaw Mountain is just west of Mt. Adams. And although the Great Cross Over is no more, there is a bridge across the Columbia River in that very spot. Every day hundreds of cars, trucks, and bicycles cross between Washington and Oregon on the Bridge of the Gods, which opened in 1926.

holding a single tree above the water. Others are home to large communities.

West of the sound is the Olympic Peninsula, an upthrust fist of

After being tossed in the surf like toys, giant trees rest on western Washington's miles of Pacific beaches.

mountains whose jagged, snow-sprinkled knuckles form Seattle's sunset skyline. A smaller peninsula, the Kitsap, juts like a thumb from the Olympic peninsula into Puget Sound. The highest peak in the Olympic Mountains is Mount Olympus, at nearly eight thousand feet. When its veil of clouds lifts, Olympus is visible from Vancouver Island, a part of Canada separated from the Olympic Peninsula by a waterway called the Strait of Juan de Fuca.

South of the dramatic Olympic Peninsula is the gentler landscape of

LAND AND WATER

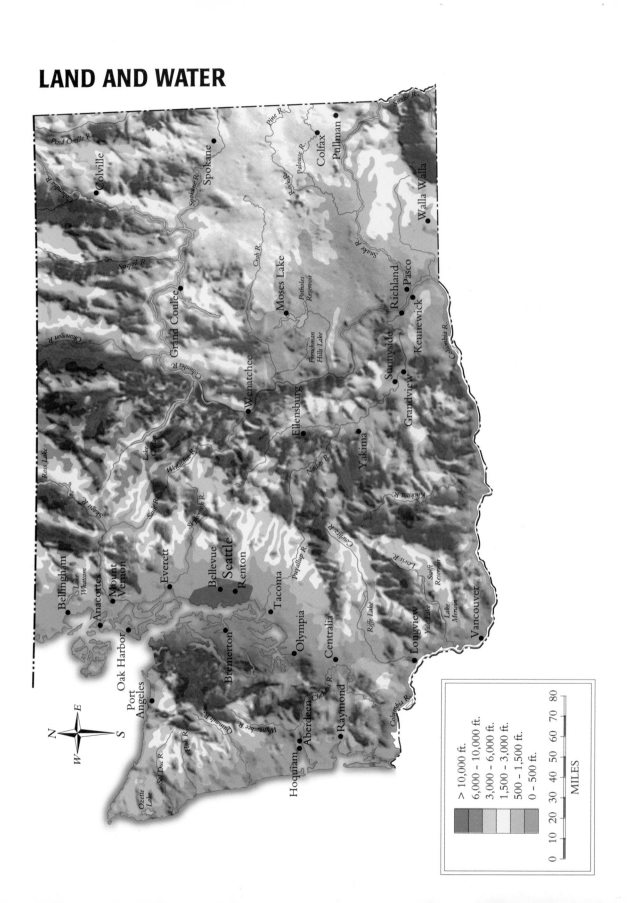

Pend Oreille R.

Colville

Columbia R.

Sanpoil R.

Ross Lake

Okanogan R.

Skagit R.

Sauk R.

Bellingham

Lake Whatcom

Anacortes

Mount Vernon

Oak Harbor

Port Angeles

Elwha R.

Sol Duc R.

Ozette Lake

Hoh R.

Queets R.

Quinault R.

Wynoochee R.

Hoquiam

Aberdeen

Chehalis R.

Raymond

Bremerton

Olympia

Centralia

Everett

Bellevue Seattle
Renton

Tacoma

Skykomish R.

Snoqualmie R.

Lake Chelan

Wenatchee R.

Spokane R.

Spokane

Crab R.

Moses Lake

Grand Coulee

Wenatchee

Columbia R.

Ellensburg

Yakima

Naches R.

Klickitat R.

Cowlitz R.

Lewis R.

Swift Reservoir

Longview

Yale Lake

Lake Merwin

Vancouver

Riffe Lake

Puyallup R.

Chehalis R.

Columbia R.

Pine R.

Palouse R.

Rock R.

Colfax

Pullman

Snake R.

Snake R.

Walla Walla

Richland

Pasco

Kennewick

Sunnyside

Grandview

Columbia R.

Potholes Reservoir

Frenchman Hills Lake

N
E
S
W

> 10,000 ft.
6,000 - 10,000 ft.
3,000 - 6,000 ft.
1,500 - 3,000 ft.
500 - 1,500 ft.
0 - 500 ft.

0   10   20   30   40   50   60   70   80

MILES

southwestern Washington. Ranges of hills with quiet farming valleys nestled between them stretch down to the bays and beaches of the coast. In the far southwest is Long Beach Peninsula, a twenty-eight-mile strip of sand lined with piles of salt-stained driftwood washed ashore over the years by the ceaseless wind and waves.

CLIMATE AND WEATHER

"Washington has two completely different climates," says Seattle weather scientist Doug McCleary. "Our weather machine has two main parts—the Pacific Ocean and the Cascade Mountains." Powerful winds from the Pacific blow moisture toward Washington. When the moisture hits land, it falls as rain or snow. Onrushing clouds get stuck against the Olympic Mountains and drop their moisture there, making the west side of the Olympic Peninsula the wettest part of Washington. Some places average 135 inches of rain a year.

But plenty of moisture makes it past the Olympics. The Puget Sound Lowland—including Seattle, Washington's largest city—gets about forty inches of rain a year. Most of it falls between October and April in frequent drizzles that can go on for days. "It gets kind of weird," admits teenager Kariah Mills, who moved to Seattle from Michigan. "It's not very cold here in the winter, which is nice, but sometimes I really miss the sun. Day after day of gray skies can drive you crazy. And people here don't use umbrellas. It's like they're trying to pretend it's not raining." That's exactly what they're doing, according to seventeen-year-old Jackson Rewell, who has spent his whole life in Seattle, not worrying about the rain.

"Don't go camping without a book or a deck of cards," advises a Washingtonian. "You'll need something to do when it rains."

"You just have to ignore it and get on with your life," he advises. "Sports, hanging out, whatever you want to do. What's the worst that can happen? You get wet."

The western slopes of the Cascades catch a lot of rain and snow. Some years Mount Rainier gets more than a thousand inches of snow, and highways through the mountains are frequently closed in winter. But east of the mountains, some places are almost deserts. Parts of the Columbia Plateau get only six inches of rain and snow a year.

Coastal Washington is warmer in the winter and cooler in the summer than places farther inland. That's because moist air blowing in from the Pacific keeps temperatures from reaching extremes. Seattle has an average midwinter temperature of 41 degrees Fahrenheit and a midsummer temperature of 66 degrees. But east of the Cascades, where the air is dryer, temperatures have plunged as low as -48 degrees Fahrenheit in winter and risen to a broiling 120 degrees in summer.

Having one climate west of the mountains and another in the east gives Washingtonians some variety. During winter, people from the east side can come to the cloudy, moist west side for relief from the bitter cold of the plateau, while west-siders desperate for a glimpse of the sun can spend a weekend happily shivering in the bright but chilly interior.

WILD WASHINGTON

Trees once covered more than half of Washington. Large areas have been cut to clear farmland or to harvest timber, but enough of the state remains forested to earn it the nickname the Evergreen State.

Most of Washington's trees are evergreens—trees that do not shed their leaves in the fall. The dry east side has forests of ponderosa pine, especially in the mountainous north. It also has big, treeless stretches of high-prairie vegetation, such as mile upon mile of sweet-scented gray-green sagebrush. The state tree, the western hemlock, grows all over Washington, as does the Douglas fir. The largest trees and densest forests are in the western Cascades and the Olympics, where dark green ferns and moss dripping with moisture form a lush undergrowth beneath the high canopies of western red cedar and Sitka spruce.

Flowers are one of Washington's glories. More than three thousand kinds of wildflowers grow in the state. Mountain meadows and eastern roadsides blaze with pink fireweed, red Indian paintbrush, purple lupines, and yellow poppies. One of the most spectacular flowering plants is the coast rhododendron, the state flower. This bush's leaves are glossy green all year long, and its springtime blooms are white, red, yellow, pink, or orange.

Wild creatures are plentiful in Washington. Black bears, elk, and deer live in most large forests. Shaggy, white, nimble-footed mountain goats live among some high crags, and mountain lions dwell in the Cascades and the Olympics. Coyotes, bobcats, beavers, foxes, otters, and raccoons are native to much of the state.

The bald eagle is one of the hundreds of kinds of birds that live in Washington or pass through it while migrating. Several hundred eagles spend time along the Skagit River north of Seattle, and in late winter people take boat trips to watch them gather in trees and snatch fish from the water. On the east side, bird-watchers flock to the Columbia National Wildlife Refuge in Othello to see a rare colony of sandhill cranes, tall, gangly birds that dance to attract mates. "Washington is a birder's paradise," a bird-watcher from Everett proclaims. "One year I even saw snowy owls from Alaska feeding along the coast."

Washington's best-known sea creatures may be orcas, black-and-white whales that frolic in Puget Sound and the Strait of Juan de Fuca. People on the ferryboats that run between the mainland and the islands sometimes see these mighty mammals leaping from

Mountain goats still scramble from rock to rock on some of Washington's peaks.

Orcas are hunters, but these magnificent whales have never been known to attack humans.

the water. Gray whales cruise the deeper offshore waters. Washington's rivers and seas are home to many varieties of salmon and trout. Clams, oysters, crabs, and lobsters live in the coastal waters. "Puget Sound is an underwater wonderland," says Bill Sayre, a scuba-diving instructor. "I've dived all around the world, and no place is better than here. The water is cold, but you see so many wonderful things. Especially the octopuses. They're everywhere, big ones, small ones. I've even seen them living in old bottles. They are shy, smart, and fascinating to watch."

ENVIRONMENTAL ISSUES

Washingtonians face some urgent environmental issues. One involves the timber industry, which has been a big part of the economy for most of the state's history. Years of clear-cutting—stripping every tree from a section of land—have left Washington's hillsides checkerboarded with large, bare patches of stumps. Many clear-cuts scar the state's national forests, right up to the borders of Olympic and Rainier National Parks.

Environmentalists point out that even when timber companies plant new trees in a clear-cut, they cannot reproduce a natural forest, which has trees of many ages. "Replanting clear-cuts does nothing but create tree farms," says Michael H. Hayes of Greenpeace, an environmental organization. Timber industry officials claim that clear-cutting is the most efficient method of logging and that logging means jobs.

Some of the most bitter fights have been about old-growth forests, places where the trees have never been cut. Some old-

A logger takes down a 750-year-old Douglas fir.

growth trees are more than six hundred years old. Loggers love old-growth timber for its high quality, but environmentalists want to preserve and study old-growth forests because they cannot be replaced. "Once old-growth forests are cut," Hayes points out, "they are gone forever." Timber companies are free to cut old growth on private land, although such forests have become rare.

THE GRAY GHOST RETURNS

Gray wolves, also called timber wolves, once roamed through Washington's mountains, slipping soft-footed through the forests and making the night skies ring with their clear, long-drawn howls. Then the white hunters and settlers came.

Beginning in the 1820s fur trappers carried out a busy traffic in wolf pelts. In the early 1900s the U.S. government wiped out the state's remaining wolves, which farmers and ranchers called pests. But in 1991 biologists in the North Cascades saw a pack of gray wolves. The next year a pack appeared farther south. Wildlife experts believe that wolves from Canada are slowly moving into the wilder parts of the Cascades.

Wolves are an endangered species in Washington. The law forbids people to kill or even bother them. But will wolves harm humans? Wolves disappear quickly once they sense people. "There has never been a report of a healthy wild wolf in North America seriously injuring a human being," says Ed Bangs of the U.S. Fish and Wildlife Service. "Think about Canadians—25 million of them live with 60,000 wolves, and there's never been a case where a wolf has attacked a small child in a red cape by a schoolbus stop." In other words, Little Red Riding Hood has nothing to fear if wolves reclaim their place in our northern forests.

Environmental groups try to block logging in old-growth forests on public land with lawsuits and protests. The federal government is working to create a timber policy that will satisfy both groups but has had little success.

Another pressing problem concerns salmon. Washington's waters once teemed with these fish, which spend part of their lives in freshwater streams and part in the ocean. The salmon industry created thousands of jobs on fishing boats and in canning plants. But each year wild salmon are scarcer. Dams block their migrating routes and kill as many as three-quarters of all young salmon when they try to swim to the sea. Soil runoff from clear-cuts muddies the streams where the salmon breed, preventing them from reproducing. Chemicals used on farms also make their way into the streams, poisoning the salmon. Some streams that used to produce thousands of salmon each year now produce only a few, or none at all.

As the number of salmon has gone down, the demand for them has gone up. The government now sets limits on the number of salmon taken each year. It hopes to work out a plan that will let people keep catching the fish while still saving enough to provide salmon for the future. Like the timber issue, however, the salmon problem is very difficult to solve. "Everyone knows there's a crisis, but no one knows what to do," says fisherman Tony Gonsalves. "Some people want to blow up the dams, some want to ban fishing for thirty years. The trouble is, no one knows whether any of these ideas will work."

Environmental issues often seem to turn one part of the state against another—east against west, or city dwellers against country

folk. "People in Seattle don't understand our problems," says a logger in the small town of Pateros. "They come into the mountains and see the trees and get all excited, and then they go back to their offices and condos while we hope we don't get laid off before we can buy winter coats for our kids." Lovers of forest and wildlife have realized that they cannot save the forests or the salmon until they admit that people need help, too. "My job is to bring all sides together and try to find a way for everyone to gain something," says a supervisor in the state's environmental office. "We're all in this state together, and we've got to solve its problems together."

Salmon are growing scarce—and stirring up controversy between environmentalists and fishermen.

2 LINKING PAST AND FUTURE

Washington did not become a state until 1889, long after many other states were formed. But although Washington is young in terms of statehood, it is old in other ways. People lived in Washington as early as 12,000 years ago. Since then, Native Americans, explorers, pioneers, builders, and dreamers have woven the rich pattern of Washington's human history.

THE NATIVE AMERICANS

Dozens of Indian tribes lived in Washington before white people arrived. East of the Cascades were the Nez Percé, Cayuse, Okanogan, Colville, Spokane, and Yakama. These tribes moved often, following game. They lived in pit houses—shallow holes with grass or branch roofs—or in a dwelling made of woven mats.

The men hunted deer, elk, and small game such as rabbits. The women gathered wild plants, especially sweet purple huckleberries and the nutritious root of the camas lily. But the most important food for these Indians was salmon. Using nets and traps made of poles and woven plants, they harvested salmon as the fish came up the rivers and streams to breed. The Indians feasted on fresh salmon and dried strips of fish over fires or in the sun to

A Colville Indian settlement on the Columbia River, from a painting by Paul Kane

provide food for the winter. They also made pemmican, long-lasting cakes of pounded meat, fish oil, and berries.

West of the mountains, coastal tribes such as the Makah and Quinault, as well as Puget Sound peoples such as the Duwamish, Skokomish, and Skagit, built large wooden houses and wove their clothing from strips of cedar bark. In boats hollowed from giant cedar trunks they put to sea to hunt seals and whales. Like the eastern Indians, they also ate salmon and other fish and gathered food from wild plants.

Western Washington's abundant natural resources and mild climate gave the coastal Indians a comfortable life. They used their leisure time to create beautiful totem poles of carved and painted wood and finely decorated baskets of woven cedar strips. From time to time they gathered for large feasts called potlatches, at which the host showed his wealth and generosity by giving away his possessions.

The Chinook tribe lived along the Columbia River. They were traders who served as a link between the coastal and eastern tribes, bartering shells and crafts from the coast for skins and stone tools from the interior.

THE EXPLORERS

The outside world first came to Washington in 1592, when a sea captain named Juan de Fuca spotted the waterway that now bears his name. Serious exploration did not begin until the mid-1770s, when several Spanish expeditions visited the coast. Some of the San Juan Islands in Puget Sound are still called by the names these Spaniards gave them.

The English were the next to arrive. In 1778 James Cook sailed along the coast. While Cook studied and mapped the coast, his men obtained a number of sea otter skins. Later, when Cook sailed to China, they sold these furs at high prices. Soon the fur trade was booming.

The first American vessel to arrive on the Washington coast was the *Columbia*, captained by Robert Gray. In 1792 Gray became the first white person to sail into the mouth of the great river that he named after his ship. That same year an Englishman named George Vancouver reached Washington's waters. Vancouver spent two years exploring Puget Sound, charting its islands, and naming places after his friends and crewmen—Rainier, Puget, Baker. Members of his crew spread the word about the region's beauty and abundant resources. One of them, Joseph Whidbey, called it "a country equal to any in the world."

After Gray's voyage, the United States also claimed the region. To strengthen the American claim, President Thomas Jefferson sent Meriwether Lewis and William Clark west in 1804 to explore the land between the Mississippi River and the Pacific Ocean. The Lewis and Clark expedition crossed the Rocky Mountains and

In 1792, the Columbia *became the first ship to sail into the mouth of the Columbia River.*

then followed the Snake and Columbia Rivers to the ocean. The explorers returned east with word of the rich, fertile territory they had seen along the Columbia. Soon people were turning their attention to "the Oregon country," the vast region that included present-day Oregon, Washington, and Idaho.

THE PIONEERS

The first English and American pioneers came for fur, especially the soft beaver pelts that were used to make hats and coats. These furs became so valuable during the 1800s that they were exchanged like money. A British firm called the North West Company sent men into the Oregon country to buy furs from the Indians, and in 1810 they built Spokane House, a trading post near where the city of Spokane stands today. It was the first white settlement in what is now Washington. A year later Americans built Fort Okanogan. In 1818 Great Britain and the United States agreed that people from both nations could trade and settle in the Oregon country until the question of who owned it was decided.

At first it seemed that the English would control the region. The powerful Hudson's Bay Company (HBC), an English trading firm operating in Canada, sent men into Washington in 1821. Four years later John McLoughlin built an HBC fort on the north bank of the Columbia River and named it Fort Vancouver. Although McLoughlin was supposed to look after England's interests in the Oregon country, he helped Americans get settled there. Many American pioneers owed their success—and their lives—to his good advice and generosity.

After crossing the wild continent in 1836, pioneer Eliza Spalding called Fort Vancouver—shown here in a painting by Henry Warre—"the midst of civilization, where the luxuries of life seem to abound."

Some of the first Americans to travel overland to Washington were missionaries who came to preach Christianity to the Indians. In 1836 missionaries led by Marcus and Narcissa Whitman founded an outpost near present-day Walla Walla. According to historian Roger Sale, "When they failed to convert the native people in satisfying numbers, they sought to attract American settlers to fill their pews."

The Whitman party's route across the continent soon became a highway for hundreds, then thousands of settlers who came west with wagons and livestock to start new lives and establish new communities. "People talk a lot about the Oregon Trail, or even the Oregon and California Trail," says Lynn Halsemeier, a teacher in Tacoma. "Let's not forget that that same trail also brought a lot of folks to Washington."

Fur had brought the traders, but land drew the settlers west. In many parts of the United States good farmland was already scarce and expensive, but in the Oregon country it was free to anyone willing to work and live on it. Pioneers began settling the region around Puget Sound. They founded Tumwater, Washington's first town, in 1845. Olympia came into being a year later.

By this time, the United States and Great Britain had decided to divide the Oregon country. The British wanted the Columbia River to serve as the border between British and American territory. The Americans objected. Early in the 1840s an American explorer named Charles Wilkes had studied the Pacific Northwest coast and decided that the Columbia River was too dangerous to be a useful port. Wilkes urged the U.S. government to demand a more northerly border so that Americans would control Puget Sound, with its good ports. In 1846 the two nations agreed on the border that now divides the United States and Canada.

Once the Oregon country belonged to the United States, it was more attractive than ever to American settlers. Not even tragedy slowed them down. The tragedy began with the region's Native Americans, who were dying in great numbers from diseases introduced by the whites, especially measles and smallpox. The Indians also began to fear, quite rightly, that they would be shoved off their

"It is no journey for the faint of heart," wrote one Washington pioneer. Still, thousands of families made the long, hard trip to what was then called the Oregon country.

land to make room for farms and ranches. In 1847 a band of Cayuse Indians, blaming the whites at the Whitman mission for the sicknesses among their people, attacked the mission, killing the Whitmans and a dozen others. The Cayuse War that followed pitted American settlers against Indians, but it did not discourage other Americans from following the trail west.

STATEHOOD

In 1848 Congress officially made the Pacific Northwest part of the United States by creating the Oregon Territory, with its capital at

A PIONEER WOMAN'S DIARY

Born in Maine in 1811, Mary Richardson started keeping a diary when she was twenty-two years old—and kept it for fifty-seven years. In 1838 she married Elkanah Walker, and they started out on the long and difficult Oregon Trail. Mary Richardson Walker's diary gives glimpses of life on the trail:

April 27. I feel that dangers & perils await; that we ought to realize that every day may be our last.

July 6. We were again saluted by a company on foot. . . . Their faces were painted. White men acted like Indians. It is said that many of the white men in the Mts. try to act as much like Indians as they can & would be glad if they really were so.

July 15. On our right, snow capped mountains. Saw a flock of antelopes. Last night a large band of buffalow passed so near we could hear them pant. Fell in with a company of Snakes [Indians]. Encamped to trade with them.

August 25. We descended a longer hill than I ever walked down before. Connor's wife [had a baby]. At noon she collected fuel & prepared dinner. Gave birth to a daughter before sunset.

August 29. Left baggage behind, and hasten on. Arrived at Dr. Whitman about two p.m. . . . Just as we were sitting down to eat melons, the house became thronged with Indians & we were obliged to suspend eating and shake hands with some 30, 40, or 50 of them. Towards night we partook of a fine dinner of vegetables, salt salmon, bread, butter, cream, &c. Thus our long toilsome journey at length came to a close.

Salem in present-day Oregon. Two years later the government counted a total of 13,000 Americans living in the territory. Less than one-tenth of them lived in what is now Washington.

Although their numbers were small, the dwellers north of the Columbia River were eager to have their own government, for they did not like having to cross the river and travel south to Salem for all official business. They asked Congress to make their region into a separate territory called Columbia. In 1853 Congress created the new territory but named it Washington in honor of the first president.

The new territory was already growing fast, thanks to its trees. Pioneers marveled at the size of the mighty forest giants of western Washington. Years later they told of trees so big that eight couples could dance atop the stumps after the trees were cut down. Timber was in demand in many places around the world, and ships could easily access harbors in Puget Sound to load it. Sawmills were soon humming and clattering around the sound. Towns such as Tacoma grew up around the mills.

In 1851 a group of pioneers founded a settlement that they named Seattle in honor of a local Suquamish Indian chieftain. Seattle, or Sealth, is a figure of some mystery. Because his people did not keep written records, we know only legends about his early life. He is best remembered for a stirring speech that he made in 1854. "My people are few," it went. "They resemble the scattering trees of a storm-swept plain. . . . Our people are ebbing away like a rapidly receding tide that will never return. . . . The Red Man has ever fled the approach of the White Man, as the morning mist flees before the morning sun."

Dwarfed by the tall, dark forests, early settlers believed that the supply of trees was endless.

Seattle's speech was a majestic tribute to the Indians' sorrow at the loss of their way of life. The only trouble is that we have no exact record of what he really said. The Puget Sound Indians spoke in blunt, direct sentences, not in the flowery, poetic language favored by American writers in the 1800s. Seattle may have expressed the ideas contained in the speech, but the language came from an American doctor named Henry Smith, who heard the speech, took notes on it, and published his version more than thirty years later.

In 1855 the government placed the Puget Sound tribes on reservations. Seattle spent his last days trying to protect his people on their reservation. The chieftain died in 1866 and was buried in Suquamish on the Kitsap Peninsula. From his grave you can look across Puget Sound to Seattle, the largest city in North America named for an Indian.

Although Indians in eastern Washington continued to resist being moved off their land and onto reservations into the 1870s, white settlers took control of the area anyway. Many were ranchers who grazed cattle and sheep on the plains. Farmers knew that eastern Washington, with its good soil and plentiful sunshine, would be excellent farming country—if only it was not so dry. By the 1890s people had begun irrigating, channeling river water through their fields. Soon the region was producing wheat and apple crops.

By that time the town of Spokane was flourishing near the site of the old fur-trading post. It soon became Washington's second-largest city. Spokane was a hub of the "inland empire"—the mining, logging, ranching, and farming region that included eastern Washington and Oregon, Idaho, and Montana.

Railroads changed the landscape and boosted industry all over the country in the late 1800s. In 1883 the Northern Pacific Company completed a railroad connecting Puget Sound with the East Coast. How important were the trains? The people of Tacoma were so happy to have the railroad come to their city that a new business district sprang up near the site chosen for the tracks and station. The people of Yakima were so upset when the track passed north of their town instead of through it that they lifted all the buildings in town and moved them to the railroad line. All across Washington, new towns sprang up along the tracks.

People discovered that it was a lot easier to get to Washington by railroad than by wagon. By 1889 the territory had more than 300,000 inhabitants. That year Washington became the nation's forty-second state.

The railroads arrived in Washington in the 1880s, shortening the journey west from the Mississippi River from five months to five days.

MODERN WASHINGTON

At the turn of the century, Seattle had a surge of growth spurred by events thousands of miles way. Miners found gold in Canada's Klondike region. The first shipload of the precious metal arrived in Seattle in 1897. When word got out, the Klondike gold rush was on. People from all around the world swarmed to Seattle, fighting to get places on ships headed for Alaska, the gateway to the Klondike. Business in Seattle boomed as merchants sold supplies to the hopeful prospectors.

The growing timber industry fed the boom, employing two out of every three working Washingtonians. But the life of the lumberjack was not easy. As writer Doug Honig says, "Logging was strenuous physical labor performed outdoors in the rain. . . . After a ten-hour day in the woods, lumberjacks trudged back in wet clothes to crowded, boxlike shacks with neither showers nor drying rooms. . . . The lumberjacks' biggest gripes concerned sleeping conditions. Camps often provided neither blankets nor mattresses, but simply hard pallets with perhaps a bit of straw."

Workers' demands for improved conditions, shorter hours, and better pay steered Washington toward liberal leaders who tried to help ordinary people and give them a greater voice in government. Washington also showed its progressive side in 1910, when it became the fifth state to give women the right to vote.

Washington contributed ships, timber, wheat, and about 70,000 servicemen and women to the United States' war effort during World War I, which ended in 1918. Although prosperity followed the war, the good times ended in 1929, when the United States

ACRES OF CLAMS

The melody of "Acres of Clams" comes from an Irish song about a wandering fiddler, "Rosin the Beau." This same tune has been used many times over with different sets of words. It was a favorite in nineteenth-century presidential campaigns, notably in 1860, as "Lincoln and Liberty."

For one who gets riches by mining,
Perceiving that hundreds grow poor,
I made up my mind to try farming,
The only pursuit that is sure.

Chorus: The only pursuit that is sure,
(2 times)
I made up my mind to try farming,
The only pursuit that is sure.

So, rolling my grub in a blanket,
I left my tools on the ground.
And I started one morning to shank it
For the country they call Puget Sound.

Chorus: For the country . . .

Arriving flat broke in midwinter,
The ground was enveloped in fog;
And covered all over with timber
Thick as hair on the back of a dog.

Chorus: Thick as hair . . .

When I looked at the prospects so
gloomy
The tears trickled over my face;
And I thought that my travels had
brought me
To the end of the jumping-off place.

Chorus: To the end . . .

I staked me a claim in the forest
And set myself down to hard toil.
For two years I chopped and I strug-
gled,
But I never got down to the soil.

Chorus: But I never . . .

I tried to get out of the country,
But poverty forced me to stay.
Until I became an old settler,
Then nothing could drive me away.

Chorus: Then nothing . . .

And now that I'm used to the country,
I think that if man ever found
A place to live easy and happy,
That Eden is on Puget Sound.

Chorus: That Eden . . .

No longer the slave of ambition.
I laugh at the world and its shams;
As I think of my happy condition,
Surrounded by acres of clams.

Chorus: Surrounded by acres . . .

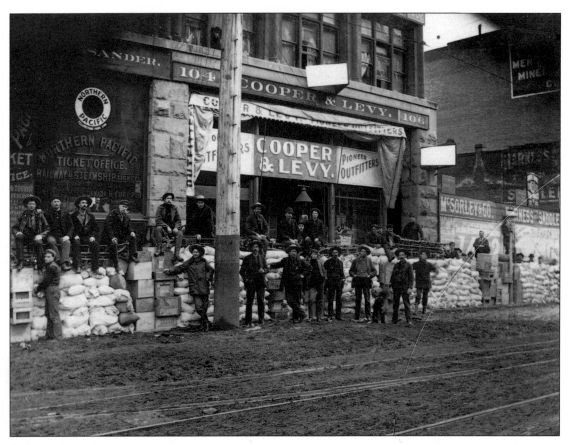

Seattle's stores overflowed with supplies to feed fortune seekers during the Klondike gold rush.

entered the Great Depression, a period of worldwide economic trouble. As part of a program to give work to the jobless, the federal government employed thousands of Washingtonians on two immense construction projects: the Bonneville Dam, completed in 1937, and the Grand Coulee Dam, completed in 1941.

That same year the United States entered World War II, which brought many changes to Washington. Some of the changes seemed good. The demand for war materials supported new industries.

Shipyards were busy, and thousands of people from around the country found jobs in new plants making airplanes and aluminum.

Other changes were not so good. The government built a top-secret military plant at Hanford in central Washington. Workers there made the plutonium that was used in an atomic bomb dropped on Japan. Years later, people would learn that leaks of deadly radiation from Hanford were responsible for sicknesses in the area. "The government had no right to do what it did to us,"

The plentiful supply of timber and the demands of two world wars created a thriving shipbuilding industry around Puget Sound.

says Aileen Warren, whose family lived in nearby Richland at the time. "It treated people like lab rats."

World War II brought disaster to Japanese Americans in Washington and all along the West Coast. Fearing that these people might secretly work for Japan, America's enemy in the war, the federal government rounded them up and forced them to spend the war years in "camps" far from their homes. These camps were really prisons, surrounded by barbed wire and armed guards. Although many Americans of Japanese descent lost everything when they were uprooted from their homes, some managed to rebuild their lives. Junkoh Harui's family had owned a plant nursery on Bainbridge Island since the early 1900s. When the family had to leave during the war, the gardens fell to ruin. People stole most of the plants. But a few seedlings that Harui's father planted just before leaving are now strong, sixty-foot pines. "My parents had what is called *gaman*—inner strength, the strength to persevere," Harui says. "It's a great legacy for us."

The second half of the 1900s brought continued growth to Washington. A world's fair in Seattle in 1962 and another in Spokane in 1974 drew attention to the state. People began to speak of Washington as a great place to live—safe, clean, uncrowded, and bursting with natural beauty. New industries such as electronics manufacturing, software design, and biotechnology research continue to lure people to the Puget Sound area. Others come to Washington for the mild climate, the scenery, or the relaxed, outdoorsy way of life. The state's population and economy seem likely to keep growing—and Washingtonians new and old hope that they can keep their state Evergreen.

"The Space Needle is our symbol of the future," said a proud member of
Seattle's city council during the 1962 world's fair.

3 HOW IT WORKS

A fountain near the capitol in Olympia

Like other states and the United States as a whole, Washington has a constitution that allows people to elect the government. The constitution also tells Washingtonians how they can create laws, settle disagreements, and make decisions about their state. The constitution dates from 1889, but it moves forward with the times. Citizens can vote to change or expand it.

INSIDE GOVERNMENT

Washington's government operates from offices in Olympia, the state capital. The government has three divisions: the executive, legislative, and judicial branches.

Executive. The executive branch is responsible for seeing that the state's laws are carried out and for determining how the state's income—raised from taxes—is spent. The governor, who is elected to a four-year term, appoints the heads of various departments and agencies, holds cabinet meetings with advisors and officials, and prepares the state budget. Other executive branch officials, such as the attorney general and the commissioner of public lands, oversee dozens of agencies that carry out the law in fields ranging from the environment to workplace safety.

Washington has had some notable governors. In 1997, Gary Locke became the first Chinese American to be governor of any

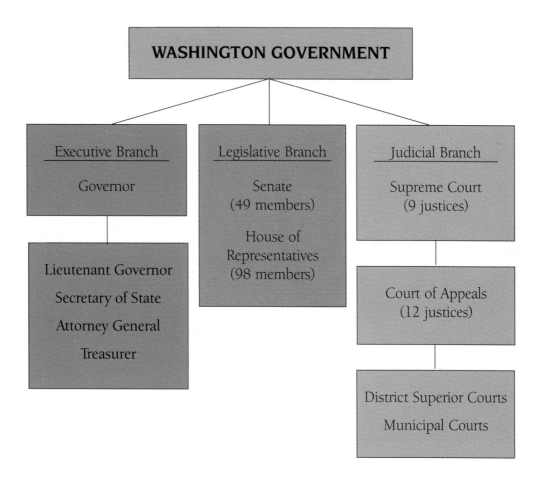

WASHINGTON GOVERNMENT

Executive Branch

Governor

Lieutenant Governor

Secretary of State

Attorney General

Treasurer

Legislative Branch

Senate
(49 members)

House of
Representatives
(98 members)

Judicial Branch

Supreme Court
(9 justices)

Court of Appeals
(12 justices)

District Superior Courts

Municipal Courts

state. When Locke was sworn into office in the handsome capitol building in Olympia, he noted that he was standing just a few blocks from where his grandfather worked as a servant. "One hundred years to travel one mile," he said. Locke believes that education is vital to maintaining a society where opportunities are open to people of all backgrounds. Education is "like electricity," he says. "People can plug into it at any time of their lives."

Legislative. The legislature is the branch of government that makes laws. It consists of a senate and a house of representatives. Washington's voters elect forty-nine senators for four-year terms

Governor Gary Locke sits atop the Great Wall during a 1997 visit to China.

and ninety-eight representatives for two-year terms. These legislators write and vote on bills. If the governor signs a bill, it becomes law. If the governor vetoes it—decides not to sign it—it will still become law if enough members of the legislature support it.

Judicial. The judicial branch applies the law through a system of courts. The justices in municipal and district courts listen to cases ranging from parking tickets to minor property damages. Serious crimes such as murder are tried in superior courts. The state supreme court decides cases that have been appealed from lower courts. In doing so, it often interprets the law in ways that affect later cases. Washington's voters elect the nine justices of the state supreme court to six-year terms.

POLITICAL ISSUES

Land use is one of Washington's hottest political issues, argued at every level from the neighborhood to the state legislature. Pointing to the sprawl of strip malls, housing developments, and parking lots that has swallowed up hundreds of square miles near Puget Sound in recent years, some land-use planners consider urban growth a monster that must be brought under control. They want to establish urban growth limits, preserve farmland and undeveloped country-side close to cities, and develop public transportation instead of building even more roads and highways. Not everyone supports these goals. "The environmentalists want us to build row houses, condos, and apartments because they take up less land," complains the owner of a Seattle-based construction company. "But most parents want their families to have a house of their own, with a yard. Shouldn't people be able to live the way they want?" Citizens in many parts of the state are getting involved in the land-use question by attending city council meetings and working to have proposals about land issues placed on ballots for voters to decide.

Crime among young people is another issue that concerns Washingtonians. People under the age of twenty-one are involved in a growing percentage of burglaries and other crimes, many of them related to drug and alcohol abuse. Schools, law enforcement agencies, churches, and concerned parents are looking for ways to keep kids out of trouble. "I work with young kids, ages eleven to fourteen," says Seattle's Jamile Wilde, who helps run after-school basketball games. "I don't preach at kids. They come here to play b-ball, not listen to someone like me tell them what to do. But I try to get the message across that, hey, we are all in this together and we have no time for drugs, fighting, or racism."

EVERGREEN STATE ECONOMY

Washington's economy is changing. In the mid-1900s most Washingtonians worked in jobs such as logging or manufacturing. Now more people are employed in service jobs, such as sales, banking, restaurant work, and the thriving tourist industry.

Trade is becoming ever more important to Washington's economy. Seattle is closer to Asia than any other seaport in the mainland United States, and Washington has become a leader in U.S. trade

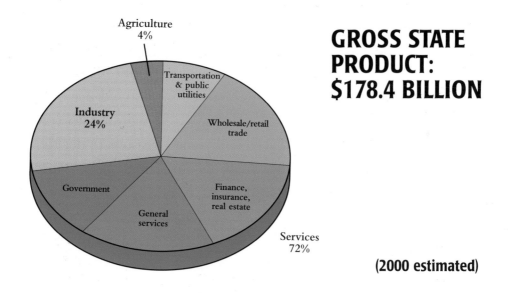

Agriculture
4%

Transportation
& public
utilities

Industry
24%

Wholesale/retail
trade

Government

Finance,
insurance,
real estate

General
services

Services
72%

GROSS STATE PRODUCT: $178.4 BILLION

(2000 estimated)

STATE FAIR

Horses, horses, horses—that's the theme of Washington's Evergreen State Fair, held each summer in Monroe, northeast of Seattle in the foothills of the Cascades. The fairgrounds contain the state's largest horseback-riding facility, which makes the fair the perfect place for events from horse shows to pony rides to a rodeo. Horses aren't the only animals at the fair, though—it features pig races, a reptile safari, and 4-H animal shows at which young people show the farm animals they have raised. Car races, logging contests, and country music round out the fun. "There's a lot to do, but sometimes I think I just come for the food," said eleven-year-old Justin White as he tried to decide between a corn dog and fried chicken at the 1996 fair.

Another large fair takes place each fall in Puyallup (pew-ALL-up). In addition to country and folk music, a famous wooden roller coaster, and other rides, the Puyallup Fair features a working farm that is designed to give kids a close-up look at animals, including llamas, piglets, goats, and sheep.

with Asia. Ports around Puget Sound bristle with loading cranes, and a glimpse of the sound likely reveals several huge cargo ships and barges carrying timber, paper, wheat, chemicals, computer software, or seafood to customers around the Pacific Rim in exchange for automobiles, electronic devices, clothing, and textiles.

The state's largest industry is producing transportation equipment. Seattle's Boeing Company is the world's leading airplane manufacturer. For years, Boeing shaped Seattle's economy. When the company did well, so did the whole region—and when the

Tugs nudge an oil tanker to a refinery pier near Anacortes. From Olympia to Bellingham, Washington's ports are among the country's busiest.

Founded in 1916, the Boeing Company produces aircraft such as these 767 jets.

company hit hard times, western Washington suffered. Between 1993 and 1995 nearly 47,000 Boeing workers lost their jobs after the company's sales fell. A turnaround came in 1996, when the company expanded and began hiring more than 50,000 new employees. Some workers remain cautious, however. "Sure, I'm glad to have a good job," says one Boeing employee. "But I knew people who got laid off in '93. It could happen to me next time." Today, however, the growing importance of other industries

EARNING A LIVING

Natural Resources

Coal

Copper — C

Gold — Au

Lead — Pb

Timber

Zinc — Z

Agriculture

Potatoes

Rye

Wheat

Dairy Products

Fruit

Onions

Barley

Beans

Beef Cattle

Industry

Aircraft Equipment

Shipbuilding

Food Processing

Paper & Wood Products

Computer Equipment

Places and Rivers

Pend Oreille R.
Colville
Columbia R.
Spokane R.
Spokane
Pine R.
Palouse R.
Rock R.
Snake R.
Colfax
Pullman
Sanpoil R.
Crab R.
Moses Lake
Potholes Reservoir
Walla Walla
Snake R.
Richland
Pasco
Kennewick
Okanogan R.
Columbia R.
Wenatchee
Frenchman Hills Lake
Ellensburg
Sunnyside
Grandview
Columbia R.
Ross Lake
Lake Chelan
Wenatchee R.
Yakima
Naches R.
Klickitat R.
Skagit R.
Sauk R.
Skykomish R.
Lewis R.
Swift Reservoir
Bellingham
Lake Whatcom
Mount Vernon
Everett
Bellevue
Seattle
Tacoma
Anacortes
Renton
Olympia
Centralia
Puyallup R.
Cowlitz R.
Riffe Lake
Yale Lake
Longview
Lake Merwin
Vancouver
Oak Harbor
Bremerton
Port Angeles
Chehalis R.
Raymond
Quinault R.
Wynoochee R.
Hoquiam
Aberdeen
Columbia R.
Sol Duc R.
Hoh R.
Ozette Lake
Grand Coulee

means that Boeing's ups and downs do not affect the region as powerfully as they once did.

Other industries vital to Washington's economy are aluminum production, shipbuilding, and electronics. The Microsoft Corporation, located in Redmond, makes the world's best-selling computer software. Washington also has a large construction industry. Rapid population and economic growth have created a high demand for new houses and other buildings.

"Some parts of this job are still pretty much like they were a hundred years ago," says a lumberjack who works along the Skagit River.

Wheat is a valuable resource of the inland empire. Washington ships much of its wheat to Asia and Russia.

Forestry—which includes logging, milling, and processing wood—is the state's third-largest industry, and agriculture is the second-largest. Key crops are apples, wheat, cherries, potatoes, raspberries, lentils, and hay. Many farms now employ fewer people than they used to because machines perform some tasks. Still, thousands of temporary or seasonal workers—many of them from Mexico—find jobs in Washington, especially picking fruit. Migrant workers live in a wide variety of conditions. Some farms provide workers with housing, although it is often shabby. But state senator Margarita Prentice points out that many migrants sleep in cars, under tarps, or in ditches. She hopes to pass laws that would make it easier for farmers to build housing for migrant workers.

Traditional jobs based on natural resources do not employ as many people as they once did. As resources become scarce and machines perform more tasks, the jobs disappear. "I'm the third generation in my family to work on the water," says a commercial

Harvesttime in the Yakima Valley means work for thousands of people.

YAKIMA APPLE PIE

Washington produces more apples than any other state in the country, and Washingtonians have almost as many ways of making apple pie as they have apples. This recipe for apple-and-cheese pie comes from an orchard owner in the Yakima Valley. She suggests using Granny Smith apples, which are juicy and not too sweet. You can make your pie crust from scratch, but "our apples are so fabulous they made store-bought crust taste good," she boasts. Have an adult help you with this recipe.

1. Preheat the oven to 450 degrees.

2. Peel and core 4 to 6 apples and cut them into thin slices. You need about 5½ cups of slices for a 9-inch crust. Put them in a large bowl.

3. In another bowl, mix ½ cup sugar (either white or brown), ⅛ teaspoon salt, 1 tablespoon cornstarch, ¼ teaspoon cinnamon, ⅛ teaspoon nutmeg. Pour this mixture over the slices and gently stir until the slices are coated.

4. Lay the slices in the crust in layers. The mound of slices should be lower than the edge of the crust around the outside and slightly higher in the center. Break 1 tablespoon of butter into small bits and sprinkle them over the mound.

5. Bake the pie for 20 minutes. While the pie is baking, grate 1 cup of cheddar cheese. Take the pie out of the oven and sprinkle the cheese over it. Set your oven to broil and cook the pie for a few minutes, until the cheese is melted, bubbly, and golden. Let the pie stand until it is cool enough to eat.

fisherman from Port Angeles on the Olympic Peninsula. "Now my son plans to study computer design. I know that's the way of the future. But," he adds, waving at the panorama of sea and sky that surrounds his boat, "it's hard to imagine him spending his life indoors."

Faced with a changing economy, some Washingtonians have found new ways to make a living on the land they love. One family owned a cattle ranch in the Methow Valley, a stunning sliver of pasture tucked into the gray crags of the North Cascades. No longer able to make money from the ranch, they risked losing their land. Then they decided to turn it into a resort for campers. "We built old-style bunkhouses, very simple," says the proud owner. "We did most of the work ourselves. Then we just started advertising. We raise llamas as pack animals for backpacking trips into the mountains, we have horseback-riding camps for kids in the summer, and in the winter we have people who come here for the cross-country skiing. We're not making a fortune, but we're getting by."

4 LIVING IN THE NORTHWEST

"**M**y parents don't like to tell people we're from California," says a fifteen-year-old boy whose family has lived in Seattle for less than a year. "I guess some people here blame Californians for the city getting more crowded and prices going up, and stuff like that. But the kids in my school think it's cool that I moved here from L.A. Half of them came from somewhere else, too."

Washington is growing quickly. About 4.8 million people lived in the state in 1990. By 1995 that number had increased to 5.4 million. Much of that growth was due to people moving from other states, drawn by Washington's reputation as one of the nation's best places to live.

A CHANGING ETHNIC LANDSCAPE

Washington has less ethnic diversity than many states, although that is beginning to change. Most Washingtonians are white. Descendants of the pioneers are mostly of German, English, or Scandinavian ancestry. Their heritage is reflected in such places as Seattle's Ballard neighborhood, where many people from Norway, Sweden, Denmark, and Finland settled during the city's early years. The district still has many Scandinavian businesses, restaurants, and residents. "The king of Norway visited a few years ago," recalls a Ballard woman. "Now that was exciting!"

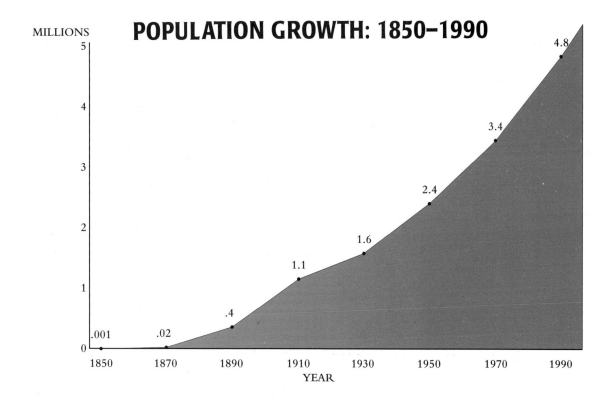

POPULATION GROWTH: 1850–1990

MILLIONS

Chinese and Japanese immigrants were also part of Washington's pioneer history. They worked on railroads and in fisheries, planted orchards, and started businesses. Today the state's Asian population is growing and becoming more varied. Veronica Kim runs a women's health program in Seattle. Her clinic's staff speaks five Chinese dialects, Korean, Tagalog (a language of the Philippines), Vietnamese, Cambodian, Thai, and Laotian. "Even good programs don't work without an interpreter who understands the culture," she says.

Washington's first significant numbers of Hispanics and African Americans arrived during World War II. Although these groups are

Generations mingle on a family farm near Ellensburg.

growing, they still make up only a small fraction of the state's population. "It's really different here," says Carla Mackie, a four-teen-year-old African American whose family moved to Seattle from the other Washington—the nation's capital. "People here are nice and all, but it's strange to see so few black faces. I feel more like a stranger."

About 100,000 Native Americans live in Washington. A third

VIKINGS ON THE SOUND

In the 1880s Norwegian settlers founded the town of Poulsbo at the head of Liberty Bay on Puget Sound—a location that resembles the narrow, winding fjords of Norway. Each year the town celebrates its Scandinavian heritage with events that draw visitors from all over the region. The Viking Fest in May features Norwegian food, entertainment, and a parade. Teams from California, Washington, Oregon, and Canada compete in the Viking Cup Invitational Soccer Tournament. Late June brings the Skandia Midsommarfest, a traditional Scandinavian celebration of the year's longest day, with folk dancing and music until the sun sets. The Fourth of July is celebrated with Fireworks on the Fjord. In early December the Yule Fest begins the holiday season in Norwegian style, with the lighting of a Yule log and the arrival of Father Christmas.

of them live on reservations, which range from the tiny Hoh reservation on the Olympic Peninsula to the sprawling Yakama reservation, the state's largest, in the south-central part of the state. The Indians have made a strong effort in recent years to reclaim their cultural heritage. In the late 1980s Cecilia Eli of the Yakama reservation lamented the fact that ten local Indian languages had been lost because reservation schools used to punish students for speaking Native American languages. Eli began teaching the traditional languages that she knew to other Indians. Her message to her students was, "Never be ashamed of what you are. No matter what

Makah Indian Stanley Black performs the Wolf Dance.

ETHNIC WASHINGTON

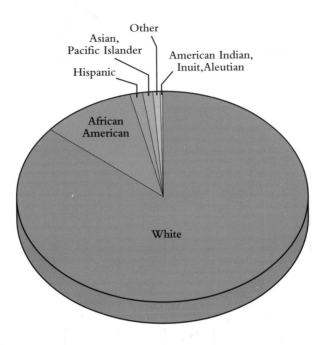

Other

Asian,
Pacific Islander

Hispanic

American Indian,
Inuit, Aleutian

African
American

White

people may call you, they cannot take away your Indian blood." Efforts such as hers may help ancient languages, customs, and beliefs to survive.

BIG CITY, SMALL TOWN, COUNTRY

Washington is unbalanced. Three-fourths of the people live in less than one-third of the state, the Puget Sound Lowland. The densest concentration of people is in the megalopolis, or supercity, that stretches ninety miles from Everett to Olympia and includes Seattle and Tacoma, the state's largest and third-largest cities.

Just as Washington's east side and west side sometimes seem to be two different states, its cities and small towns sometimes seem like two different worlds. Outside of the megalopolis, Washington

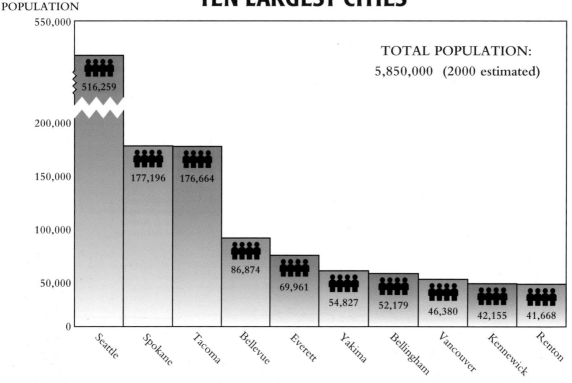

TEN LARGEST CITIES

POPULATION

TOTAL POPULATION:
5,850,000 (2000 estimated)

550,000

200,000

150,000

100,000

50,000

0

516,259
177,196
176,664
86,874
69,961
54,827
52,179
46,380
42,155
41,668

Seattle Spokane Tacoma Bellevue Everett Yakima Bellingham Vancouver Kennewick Renton

is very much a Western state. Country music plays in truck stops. Boots are everyday wear, not just for weekend hiking trips. "I laugh sometimes when I see people from Seattle come up here to camp," says a native of Skykomish, in the Cascades. "They've got fancy parkas and backpacks—six, seven hundred dollars' worth of gear to do things that my brothers and I used to do in old sneakers and sweatshirts."

Still, country life is changing in Washington, as it is everywhere. Even the most rural communities are part of the larger world, linked by television, the Internet, and highways. "I can't wait until

I'm old enough to move away from this town," declares a thirteen-year-old girl in Goldendale, near Mount Adams. "It has a great view of the mountain, but how many times can you look at a mountain?"

Some small communities are getting new residents—people who are leaving the big cities for a more relaxed, uncrowded way of life. "Now I can only spend about one week a month there," says Seat-

Seattle's skyscrapers rise glittering from the shores of Puget Sound. "It stuns me how this city's grown in my lifetime," says a 67-year-old lifelong resident.

Bavarian costumes and dances are part of Leavenworth's Oktoberfest, a German-style fall festival.

tlite Gary Banasek, who is building a house near North Cove on the Olympic Peninsula. "But if things go right at my job, I'd like to live in the country full-time and do my work by computer."

As Washington's economy shifts from resource-based industries to services and trade, many small towns have faced economic disaster. Some have turned to tourism to stay alive. Leavenworth led the way. In the 1960s this little mountain community was on the verge of becoming a ghost town. Citizens rebuilt the town, turning it into a reproduction of a traditional village in Bavaria, in southern Germany. Today its shops and resorts draw many visitors, with the festival of Christmas lights the high point of the year. "Sure, the German thing is a gimmick," admits one local teenager. "But it worked. And it's kind of fun."

RECREATION AND THE ARTS

Washington offers a world of possibilities for the outdoors enthusiast. Many Washingtonians spend as much time as they can hiking, camping, sailing, kayaking, scuba diving, mountain or rock-climbing, skiing, snowboarding, and snowmobiling. Every year hundreds participate in the two hundred-mile Seattle-to-Portland Bicycle Classic. One popular pastime is traveling among the San Juan Islands by ferryboat, with a bicycle or kayak for up-close exploration.

"When people here ask what you do, they don't want to know about your job," says a twenty-four-year-old New York City woman who recently moved to Seattle. "They want to know what sports you're into. My first week on the job, someone said to me, 'Bring your skis to the office on Friday and we'll go skiing after work.' Skis? I was embarrassed to tell them I never go outside except to walk my dog. There are people here who don't even have furniture, but they have sport utility vehicles loaded with kayaks and bikes and tents. I guess if I'm going to fit in here, I'd better learn to love the great outdoors."

White-water kayaking on the Skykomish River is not for the timid.

"Boarding rules!" cry young snowboarders. In recent years they've begun to outnumber skiers on some Washington slopes.

Washington is also famous for its arts. One of the state's best-known artist is Dale Chihuly, whose brilliantly colored glass creations are admired around the world. Crafts influenced by Native American arts, such as beadwork, basketry, and wood carving, are also widely practiced in Washington. Fairs all over the state display the work of painters, jewelers, woodworkers, and potters. Dozens of festivals celebrate the arts, most notably

Glass artist Dale Chihuly with Persian Pergola, *one of his works*

Bumbershoot, Seattle's annual arts fair, which includes dance, comedy, and theater performances.

Washington's calendar is crammed full with other fairs and festivals. Some celebrate the state's agricultural bounty by featuring apples, berries, or tulips. Eatonville's Slug Festival honors the underappreciated banana slug (a large, shell-less snail) with slug races and a slug puppet theater.

Ethnic pride is the theme of many annual events, ranging from the all-Indian rodeo in Toppenish, in central Washington, to the Black Pioneer Picnic in Roslyn, a tiny town in the Cascades. In 1997 more than 20,000 people attended a celebration of Tet, the Vietnamese New Year, held by Vietnamese students in Seattle. Quang-Trung Pham, one of the organizers, expressed the feelings of young people from many backgrounds who take part in such traditional celebrations: "This is the first time that the younger generations have taken the responsibility to organize the most important festival in Vietnamese culture. It doesn't matter where we are, be it Paris or America, it's our culture we have to preserve."

PROBLEMS AND PROMISES

"Do you know that old saying: Be careful what you wish for? That's what life here in Washington is like," says a woman who lives in Issaquah, east of Seattle. "I grew up not far from here, and it was all farms. There was only one place to shop. It seemed like a big hassle to go anywhere. You knew all your neighbors and it was boring. Now Seattle's practically on our doorstep, and I don't know if I like it."

Many Washingtonians feel the same way. Their state is changing rapidly—but is it changing for the better or the worse? Seattle is a city trying to keep its balance in a whirlwind of growth that threatens to knock it off its feet. "When we moved here in the '70s," says one resident, "I thought we had discovered the last perfect place—a wonderful city with no problems. Now we have litter, graffiti, gangs. . . . And don't even get me started about the traffic!"

Yet to many people, Seattle and Washington are proof that cities and states can grow and change without losing the qualities that make them special. Seattle is still one of the cleanest and safest

"No matter how much things change in Washington, the beach and the waves will always be here," says beachcomber and surfer Cliff Cordoba.

cities of its size in the country. And Washington still offers residents and visitors remarkable scenery, a rich and varied cultural life, and as many recreational opportunities as any place in the world. Norman Rice, mayor of Seattle from 1990 to 1997, summed up the challenges facing his city and state this way: "We've grown, we will continue to grow, and as we grow we will learn together. Washington can be the place that people look to when they want to see how to make the future work."

5 FAMOUS NAMES AND FACES

Washington's abundance of natural resources has been matched by the richness of its human resources. In politics, sports, business, and the arts, Washingtonians have made their mark. Some famous Washingtonians and their achievements have been revolutionary, unusual, or just plain odd—not bad qualities for a state whose people pride themselves on being independent.

THINKERS AND ARTISTS

Journalist and social activist Anna Louise Strong was a brilliant student who received her Ph.D. at age twenty-three. Strong was born in Nebraska in 1885 and moved to Seattle in 1915, where she became deeply involved in social causes, including the fight for workers' rights and a movement to keep the United States out of World War I. She was the first woman elected to the city's school board, but the board threw her out because of her political opinions, which other members regarded as dangerously liberal. Then America entered the war in Europe, shattering Strong's hopes for peace. "I turned like a wounded beast to the hills for shelter," she wrote. "Like the pioneers of old I fled to the simpler wilderness from the problems of human society that I could no longer face." She became a guide on Mount Rainier.

After the war Strong became a world traveler, always drawn to

A passionate believer in social change, Anna Louise Strong helped organize Seattle's general strike of 1919, when workers left their jobs to demand better pay and working conditions.

lands in turmoil. Her books revealed her sympathy for the socialists and communists who were trying to build new societies in Russia and China. These views eventually made Strong unpopular in the United States, and she spent much of her adult life abroad. In 1958 she moved to China, where she died. Modern readers can taste her love of adventurous travel and her political passions in books such as *Red Star in Samarkand* and *China's Millions*.

Jacob Lawrence was already famous when he moved to Washington: at age twenty-four, he had become the first African-American artist to have his work bought by New York City's Museum of Modern

"I don't consider myself a black painter," Jacob Lawrence once said. "I am a painter who just happens to be a black man."

Art. Lawrence was born in Atlantic City, New Jersey, in 1917, and grew up in Harlem, a black district in New York. His breakthrough came with a series of sixty paintings called *The Migration of the Negro*, which told the story of the movement of southern blacks into the northern cities. His vivid, colorful paintings draw on his experience of the sufferings and joys of ordinary people. "I paint the things I've known and experienced in my lifetime," he explained. In 1970 Lawrence arrived in Seattle to teach art at the University of Washington. He did so for more than a decade while still painting and exhibiting his own works.

GOVERNMENT AND BUSINESS

Although born in Minnesota, U.S. Supreme Court justice William

O. Douglas grew up in Yakima. "In the early years of the century when we first moved to Yakima," he wrote, "the land around town was mostly bleak sagebrush, occupied only by jackrabbits and rattlesnakes." But on the horizon loomed the green-and-white mountains. Mount Rainier won a special place in Douglas's heart, filling him with a lifelong love of the wilderness.

Douglas became a lawyer and earned his place in history by serving for thirty-six years on the Supreme Court. Driven by his belief in what he called "equality as the dominant American

Supreme Court justice William O. Douglas called the Washington Cascades "some of the finest, wildest country in the world."

theme," he helped decide landmark civil rights cases, including the case that ended racial separation in public schools. He also wrote about and worked for wilderness preservation. Although Douglas worked in Washington, D.C., for most of his life he kept a home near Mount Rainier and spent as much time there as he could. Today a huge stretch of wild, mostly roadless mountainscape between Mount Rainier and Yakima is called the William O. Douglas Wilderness in his honor.

A native Seattlite born in 1955 is one of the city's most famous business leaders—and the richest person in the world, aside from royalty. William H. Gates III, better known as Bill, became fasci-

Seattle-born Bill Gates turned his hobby into one of the world's most successful businesses.

nated with computers at age twelve. Eight years later he dropped out of Harvard University to start a software company called Microsoft with a computer-loving friend named Paul Allen. Gates and Allen believed that computers, which at that time were used only by businesses and government, were on the verge of becoming available to home users. "We realized that the revolution might happen without us," Gates has explained. "There was no question of where our life would focus."

Today, Gates's Windows system is used in the majority of the world's personal computers, and Microsoft employs thousands of people in the Seattle area. Although his company's business practices have come under attack by business rivals and the government, Gates has emerged as a visionary who was right when he predicted, "Computers will change the way we live, work, and play."

POPULAR HEROES

In the three years before his drug-related death in 1970, James Marshall "Jimi" Hendrix became one of the most famous popular musicians in the world. Born in Seattle, Hendrix began playing guitar in high school. "He listened to every kind of musical expression and idea," wrote his biographer David Henderson. "He became the best R&B and rock 'n' roll guitarist in Seattle." After a few years, Hendrix burst onto the national music scene with colorful clothes, powerful songs like "Purple Haze" and "Hey, Joe," and wild, inspired guitar-playing that, many people believe, has never been equaled. He helped black musicians break into main-

Guitar legend Jimi Hendrix got his start playing in clubs in Seattle. In more recent years the city's music scene has produced such groups as Nirvana and Pearl Jam.

stream rock music and inspired many later singers, composers, and guitarists.

Ken Griffey Jr., known to sports broadcasters and fans as Junior, is one of modern baseball's heroes. Griffey grew up around base-ball—his father was also a great player. "The only thing Dad ever

KENNEWICK MAN

One of the most famous people in Washington today lived about 9,300 years ago—but he didn't become famous until 1996, when two college students discovered his skeleton on the bank of the Columbia River near Kennewick.

Scientists were excited. Such ancient human remains are extremely rare in North America. "Kennewick Man," as he became known, offered researchers a chance to learn much more about life thousands of years ago. Not everyone shared their excitement, however. Some nearby Indian tribes wanted the U.S. Army Corps of Engineers, which now controls the skeleton, to give it to a tribe for burial. They claim that Kennewick Man is one of their ancestors. "The five tribes have come together and have all said the same thing: These remains need to go back into the ground as soon as possible," declared Armand Minthorn of the Confederated Tribes of the Umatilla.

A group of scientists has sued to keep the skeleton from being buried. They point out that it is not certain that Kennewick Man is related to any modern Indians, and they feel that the remains should be studied for what they may tell us about the early history of *all* people. The bones are "rare treasures of humanity," says scientist Amy Dansie, adding, "We share a common ground. These skeletons are important to remind everybody that we're all one people."

What will happen to Kennewick Man? A federal court will decide, although it may be years before his fate is settled.

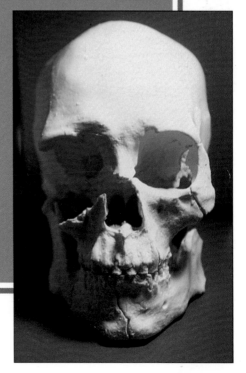

"It's outta here!" Power hitter Junior Griffey of the Seattle Mariners watches one of his home runs fly out of the ballpark.

told me was to go out and have fun, stay out of trouble and be a good kid," Griffey has said. Griffey has followed that sound advice. He began playing minor-league baseball at seventeen and joined the Seattle Mariners at age nineteen. In 1990 he and his father made baseball history as the first father and son to be teammates. Griffey's outstanding hitting and extraordinary defense have made him key to the Mariners' success, but it's his infectious enthusiasm that makes him one of the game's most popular players. Says a Mariner staff member, "Junior's the kind of guy that teammates, coaches, and fans all love. Best of all, he just really loves to play the game."

"Sick." "Twisted." "Weird." That's how some newspaper editors described the wacky cartoons that Gary Larson showed them when he was beginning his career. Larson stayed true to his own peculiar vision, however, and has become one of the most successful cartoonists of all time. "The Far Side," his world of talking cows, hungry bears, and people with strange hairdos, has appeared in newspapers around the world as well as in dozens of books and on calendars and T-shirts.

Larson, who grew up in Tacoma and now lives in Seattle, thinks that his happy childhood fed his interests and abilities. "When I was a little kid, I spent a lot of time by myself, living in my own little world," he says. He and his brother were fascinated by animals and collected a reptile menagerie that included an alligator and a boa constrictor. Larson always liked to draw, and after considering careers in science, advertising, and music he started selling cartoons. His big break came in 1979 when the *San Francisco Chronicle* made "The Far Side" a regular feature. Soon it was a global success. "People always try to look for some deep meaning in my work," Larson says. "I want to say, 'They're just cartoons, folks. You laugh or you don't.'"

6 WASHINGTON ROAD TRIP

There's a lot to see and do in the Evergreen State. Washington has three national parks, three national recreation areas, six national forests, twenty-six wilderness areas, and more than one hundred state parks, as well as one of America's most dynamic and exciting cities. Pack your bag—don't forget your raingear—and get started.

SEATTLE

Begin your tour on top of the Space Needle, the 605-foot tower that was built for the 1962 world's fair. Resembling a spaceship perched on a pole, the Space Needle is the most distinctive feature of Seattle's skyline, visible from many parts of the city. Have a meal in one of the rotating restaurants on top—every hour they spin through a complete circle. Then go out to the observation deck and enjoy the glorious view of the Olympic Mountains and Puget Sound in the west, the Cascades in the east, and Seattle spread out at your feet. From the base of the Needle you can catch the monorail. Also built for the fair, the monorail is a train that runs on a single track raised above the ground. It will whisk you downtown for more exploring.

Some Seattle landmarks are not to be missed. Pike Place Market, which opened in 1907, covers several blocks and contains dozens of stores that sell everything from jewel-bright fresh fruit to fragrant

PLACES TO SEE

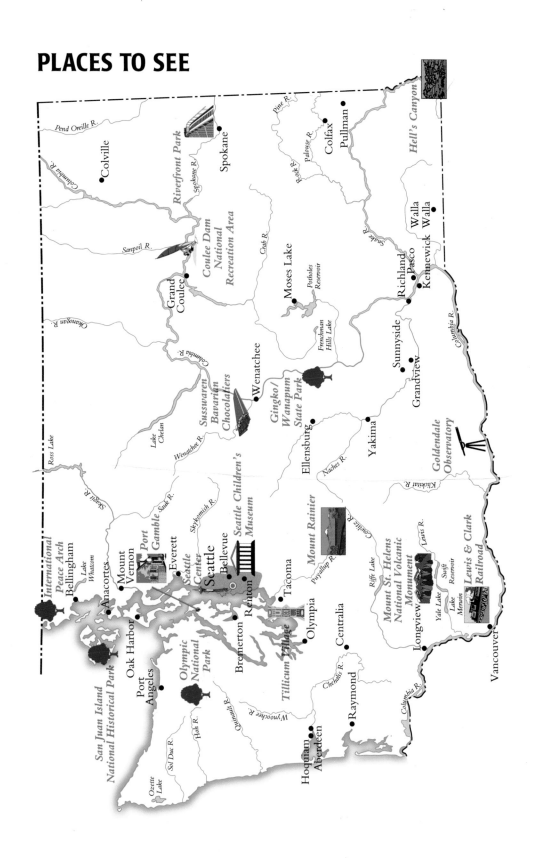

Pend Oreille R.

Colville

Columbia R.

Riverfront Park

Spokane

Pine R.

Pullman

Colfax

Palouse R.

Hell's Canyon

Rock R.

Spokane R.

Sanpoil R.

Coulee Dam National Recreation Area

Grab R.

Snake R.

Walla Walla

Okanogan R.

Grand Coulee

Moses Lake

Potholes Reservoir

Richland

Pasco

Kennewick

Columbia R.

Gingko/ Wanapum State Park

Frenchman Hills Lake

Sunnyside

Grandview

Wenatchee

Susswaren Bavarian Chocolatiers

Lake Chelan

Wenatchee R.

Ellensburg

Yakima

Naches R.

Goldendale Observatory

Ross Lake

Klickitat R.

Skagit R.

Sauk R.

Seattle Children's Museum

Skykomish R.

Port Gamble

Mount Vernon

Everett

Seattle Center

Bellevue

Seattle

Mount Rainier

Cowlitz R.

Lewis & Clark Railroad

Lewis R.

International Peace Arch

Bellingham

Lake Whatcom

Anacortes

Oak Harbor

Renton

Tacoma

Puyallup R.

Mount St. Helens National Volcanic Monument

Swift Reservoir

Yale Lake

Lake Merwin

Bremerton

Olympia

Centralia

Longview

Vancouver

Riffe Lake

San Juan Island National Historical Park

Port Angeles

Olympic National Park

Tillicum Village

Chehalis R.

Raymond

Columbia R.

Wynoochee R.

Quinault R.

Hoh R.

Sol Duc R.

Hoquiam

Aberdeen

Ozette Lake

beeswax candles to locally made handicrafts. Watch out when you pass one of the fish stalls, though—the workers there are famous for throwing fish through the air. "Never hit a customer yet!" they boast.

Rebuilt after a fire destroyed most of downtown Seattle in 1889, Pioneer Square contains many of the city's oldest buildings, as well as a giant totem pole and a statue of Chief Seattle. Here you can take a tour of Seattle's Underground, which was created during reconstruction after the fire. To make the neighborhood's hills less steep, Seattlites raised the level of the streets by roofing over the old sidewalks and stores and building above them. Some below-street-level buildings remained in use as taverns and gambling houses until the 1930s. Today's Underground, spooky but safe, is considerably tamer than in the wild "sin city" of former times.

A giant troll lives under Seattle's Aurora Bridge—in statue form. Posing in its lap for photographs is popular with many visitors. Not far away is another famous statue, *Waiting for the Interurban*. It depicts a group of life-size people waiting to catch a trolley. Often the statues wear hats, clothes, or costumes arranged by prankish local residents.

Seattle has a number of excellent museums, but if you can see only one, make it the Burke Museum on the University of Washington campus. It is famous for its exhibits of the Northwest's natural wonders, including dinosaur bones, and of Native American art and culture. You can also experience Indian culture at the Tillicum Northwest Coast Indians Cultural Center on Blake Island, a forty-five-minute boat ride from Seattle. There Indians perform traditional dances, serve salmon baked in the Native American style, and maintain a museum.

You could spend many days absorbing all that Seattle has to offer, but the rest of the state is waiting. Head north along the sound. A bridge will take you to Whidbey Island, and from there you can take a ferry to the other San Juan Islands, Washington's watery playground. The islands are a world of villages and inns, salt breezes, seafood dinners, and blue horizons. Visit San Juan Island National Historical Park near the town of Friday Harbor. You'll see the remains of English and American forts from the 1850s, when the two nations nearly went to war after an American farmer shot a British-owned pig.

TO THE EAST SIDE

The most dramatic way to go from western Washington to eastern Washington is over the North Cascades Highway. It starts in the flat, tranquil Skagit Valley, which is a red-and-yellow blaze of tulip blossoms in the spring. Then it winds up and up into North Cascades National Park, where you'll be surrounded by white glaciers, steep gray stone pinnacles, and green mountain meadows. Hours later, after a long descent through forested valleys, you'll be on the other side of the mountains.

Head south to Lake Chelan, a deep, narrow, fifty-five-mile-long gash in the mountains, carved by glaciers long ago and now full of clear, cold water. You can ride a ferry up the lake to Stehekin, an isolated, roadless community that is the starting point for backpacking adventures. Or go northeast, toward the Okanogan Highlands and the Colville Indian Reservation. Maybe you'll catch the Omak Stampede and World Famous Suicide Race, called "the most dangerous race in the world." In a seven-decade-old tradition,

Risking accident and injury, Indian riders urge their mounts on in the famous Omak Suicide Race.

Indians on horses plunge down a steep cliff and across the Okanogan River.

Don't miss Grand Coulee Dam, the largest producer of electricity in the United States. Nearly a mile long, measuring 550 feet from

Mount Shuksan towers over a lake in North Cascades National Park.

bedrock to the road across its top, Grand Coulee contains enough concrete to build a four-foot-wide sidewalk around the world—twice. "Ooh, this is the best part," said a ten-year-old visitor during the steep, scary ride in a glass elevator down into the dam to view the giant turbines and other machinery housed there. Nearby is Sun Lakes State Park, where you can see a geological marvel called Dry Falls. Its cliffs, three and a half miles wide and four hundred feet high, were the site of the world's largest waterfall several thousand years ago, before the Columbia River changed its course.

In Spokane is the Cheney Cowles Museum, site of the Eastern Washington State Historical Society. Its displays tell the story of the inland empire from dinosaur days to the railroad boom. Some exhibits feature items made by Indians from Alaska to Argentina. The Indians of the Columbia Plateau are represented by collections of clothing, beaded skin bags, and baskets made of woven corn-husks.

Leaving Spokane, travel southwest through the Palouse. The wind bends the grain and stirs the dust of empty fields, the sky looks very large above the endless rolling hills, and you can go for miles and miles without seeing another car. Along Washington's southern border you'll rejoin the Columbia River, and gradually the mountains will rise over the western horizon. As you approach Mount Adams, stop at the Maryhill Museum of Art, a mansion high on a hill overlooking the river. Peacocks roam the grounds of the museum, which contains collections of unusual chessboards, French sculptures, and items once owned by the royal family of Romania. Not far from the museum is a concrete replica of Stone-henge, England's prehistoric stone monument. The replica is a memorial to local soldiers who died in World War I.

If you're in the nearby town of Goldendale when dusk falls, visit the Goldendale Observatory. It has a twenty-four-inch telescope, one of the largest in the country open to public viewing. At night the astronomers turn the telescope to different patches of sky— the moon, the rings of Saturn, or a distant galaxy.

Spokane Falls thunders below the Monroe Street Bridge. Washington's second-largest city also has an extinct volcanic cone within its borders.

INTO THE MOUNTAINS

Heading northwest, you'll want to stop in Mount Rainier National Park as you cross the Cascades again. The park contains the Grove of the Patriarchs, a cluster of some of the largest and oldest trees in the state. It also contains Paradise, a huge old-fashioned lodge high on the mountain's flank. Rainier's smooth, ice-capped dome is even more impressive up close than on a distant skyline, but sometimes it's the small things that count. "I come here every spring for the wildflowers," says seventy-six-year-old Eileen

Red Indian paintbrush and purple lupine in a Mount Rainier meadow

The 1980 eruption swept across what is now Mount St. Helens National Volcanic Monument—but "life is slowly returning," says park ranger Noreen Bates.

Dudley Wells of Tacoma. "There are more than three hundred different kinds of wildflowers growing around this mountain, and each one is beautiful. The mountains wouldn't be complete without them. I want to see every one of 'em before I die."

Mount St. Helens National Volcanic Monument will stun you with mile upon mile of fallen trees, blasted in the 1980 eruption. You can climb to an overlook above Spirit Lake, once a Pacific

ROADSIDE ODDITIES

Washington's highways and byways sometimes offer surprises. Take Bickleton, a small town near the Columbia River in central Washington. To encourage endangered bluebirds to nest and raise families, the people of Bickleton have filled their town with a multitude of specially designed nest boxes. Or Raymond, a town of three thousand people in the southwest, which has lined the highway through town with life-size metal sculptures of deer, birds, horses and wagons, and people in pioneer-style clothing.

Some communities express themselves through murals. Wall paintings on the sides of stores and businesses depict events in the history of Long Beach, and outdoor murals display scenes from the early days in Centralia, a city founded in 1875 by black pioneer George Washington. Kalama, founded in the 1840s and named after a Hawaiian man who married a local Indian woman, has a totem pole thought to be the world's tallest. Made from a single tree, it is 140 feet high. "You really need to keep your eyes open around here," said one visitor from Pennsylvania. "You never know what's coming up."

Northwest showplace, now full of logs and mud. If you're a good hiker, you can climb a trail to the volcano's rim and peek into the steaming depths. If that doesn't sound like such a good idea, several well-designed visitors centers offer dramatic films of the eruption and information about how nature is returning life to the devastated landscape.

West of the mountains, drop in on Oysterville. This tiny town on the Long Beach peninsula in southwest Washington came into being during the mid-1800s, when oysters were plentiful in the local waters. Tradition says that the oyster-fishing industry was so prosperous that for a few years local communities had more gold than any place on the West Coast except San Francisco. Today it's a quiet backwater, perfect for walking on the beach and bird-watching.

Farther north, you can explore the Olympic Peninsula. The beaches are magnificent, but this coast is not for swimming—perils

Clam digging on the Olympic Peninsula. Washington's biggest clams, called geoducks (pronounced "gooeyducks"), can weigh five pounds or more.

include logs tossed in the waves, cold temperatures, and undertows. A trip to Olympic National Park should include a hike through the Hoh Rain Forest, which ten-year-old Nathan, a visitor from California, calls "the greenest place on Earth." This wet, lush wilderness has enormous trees, as well as the Hall of Mosses, a photographer's favorite because of its many shades of green. Continuing north and east around the peninsula, get a different view of the park from Hurricane Ridge, more than 5,200 feet above sea level. From there you'll see a panorama of peaks with Mt. Olympus in the center.

Descending from the Olympics, make your way eastward past fishing towns, campgrounds, and clear-cuts to a ferry port on the Kitsap Peninsula. Climb aboard the ferry, settle into a seat, and look east. You're headed back to where your trip began. If you're lucky, your first glimpse of Seattle will come just as night falls, and the city will be a blaze of lights reflected in the sound, with the luminous Space Needle floating above it all.

Sword ferns, moss, and bigleaf maples in the Olympic rain forest

THE FLAG: *The flag, adopted in 1923, displays the state seal on a dark green background, which symbolizes the state's forests. It was readopted in 1967 when a new portrait of Washington was chosen for the seal.*

THE SEAL: *The seal is a portrait of George Washington painted by Gilbert Stuart. Around the portrait are the words "The Seal of the State of Washington 1889." The first seal, adopted in 1889, used a likeness of Washington from a postage stamp. The Gilbert Stuart portrait replaced that likeness in 1967.*

STATE SURVEY

Statehood: November 11, 1889

Origin of Name: Named after the first American president, George Washington

Nicknames: The Evergreen State, the Chinook State

Capital: Olympia

Motto: Alki (Chinook Indian word for "by-and-by")

Bird: Willow goldfinch

Flower: Western rhododendron

Tree: Western hemlock

Fish: Steelhead trout

Gem: Petrified wood

Colors: Green and gold

Dance: Square dance

Willow goldfinch

Petrified wood

WASHINGTON, MY HOME

On February 23, 1959, at a Washington's birthday observance in the state senate, a piano was wheeled out onto the chamber floor and "Washington, My Home" was performed by a trio, including the composer, Helen Davis. The rendition brought down the house, and it was unanimously adopted as the official state song then and there.

Helen Davis

GEOGRAPHY

Highest point: 14,410 feet above sea level, at Mount Rainier

Lowest point: 5 feet below sea level, at Ebbey Island in Snohomish County

Area: 68,139 square miles

Greatest Distance, North to South: 239 miles

Greatest Distance, East to West: 370 miles

Bordering States: Idaho to the east, Oregon to the south

Hottest Recorded Temperature: 118°F at Ice Harbor Dam on August 5, 1961

Coldest Recorded Temperature: -48°F at Mazama and Winthrop on December 30, 1968

Average Annual Precipitation: 38 inches

Major Rivers: Columbia, Cowlitz, Lewis, Okanogan, Pend Oreille, Sanpoil, Skagit, Skykomish, Snake, Spokane, Yakima

Major Lakes: Chelan, Cle Elum, Crescent, Cushman, Kachess, Moses, Ozette, Quinault, Franklin D. Roosevelt, Sammamish, Soap, Washington, Wenatchee, Whatcom

Trees: alder, aspen, cottonwood, Douglas fir, lodgepole pine, maple, ponderosa pine, Sitka spruce, western hemlock, western larch, western red cedar

Wild Plants: brown-eyed Susan, everlasting lily, fern, Flett's violet, goldenrod, heather, lace, lupine, monkey flower, moss, mountain phlox, Oregon grape, piper bluebell, sagebrush, sea rose, shooting star, sunflower, western rhododendron, wild onion

Animals: badger, beaver, bobcat, clam, crab, deer, flying squirrel, gopher, marmot, marten, mink, mountain lion, mountain goat, muskrat, seal, sea lion

Mink

Birds: bald eagle, cormorant, duck, falcon, golden eagle, goldfinch, goose, gull, hawk, oystercatcher, pelican, pheasant, quail, ruffed grouse, sage grouse, sandpiper, shrike, swan, tern, turkey vulture, turnstone, vireo, waxwing, western lark

Fish: albacore tuna, cod, cutthroat trout, flounder, halibut, grayling, rainbow trout, salmon, steelhead trout, sturgeon, whitefish

Endangered Animals: Aleutian Canada goose, American peregrine falcon, bald eagle, brown pelican, Columbian white-tailed deer, green sea turtle, northern spotted owl, grizzly bear, leatherback sea turtle, marbled murrelet, gray wolf, olive turtle, Oregon silverspot butterfly, western snowy plover, woodland caribou

Gray wolf

Endangered Plants: marsh sandwort, Nelson's checker-mallow, water howellia

TIMELINE

Washington history

1700s Region inhabited by many tribes, including Nez Percé, Spokane, Yakama, Cayuse, Walla Walla, Nooksack, Chinook, Nisqually, and Quinault

1775 Spanish explorers Bruno Heceta and Juan Francisco de la Bodega y Quadra land near Point Grenville

1778 English explorer James Cook sails along coast of Washington

1791 Spanish establish colony on Neah Bay

1792 American Robert Gray discovers mouth of Columbia River; British captain George Vancouver maps the Washington coast and Puget Sound

1805 Lewis and Clark follow Columbia River to Pacific Ocean

1811 Fort Okanogan becomes first American settlement in Washington

1818 U.S. and Great Britain agree to jointly occupy Oregon region

1825 Hudson's Bay Company builds Fort Vancouver

1836 Mission founded at Waiilatpu, near Walla Walla

1840s First major wave of settlement

1846 Oregon Treaty between Britain and U.S. establishes 49th parallel as border between Washington and Canada; Olympia founded

1847 Cayuse War breaks out between Cayuse Indians and settlers

1848 Oregon Territory, which includes Washington, is created

1851 Seattle founded

1853 Washington Territory created by Congress; capital established at Olympia

1855 Discovery of gold in northeastern Washington brings rush of settlers and sparks four years of warfare between settlers and Indians

1863 Establishment of Idaho Territory gives Washington its present border

1883 Northern Pacific Railroad's cross-country line reaches Puget Sound

1885 Anti-Chinese riots in Seattle; federal troops sent in

1889 Washington becomes 42nd state

1910 Washington becomes fifth state to extend voting rights to women

1928 Capitol in Olympia is completed

1941 Grand Coulee Dam is completed

1962 World's fair held in Seattle

1976 Dixy Lee Ray is elected state's first woman governor

1979 U.S. Supreme Court upholds Indians' right to catch half the salmon returning to the waters where they traditionally fished

1980 Mount St. Helens volcano erupts, killing 57 people and causing billions of dollars in damage

1993 National environmental summit addresses tensions between loggers and environmentalists

ECONOMY

Agricultural products: apples, beef cattle, flower bulbs, milk, timber, wheat

Bulb farm

Manufactured products: airplanes, chemicals, computer equipment, food products, paper products, ships

Natural resources: clay, coal, copper, gold, lead, limestone, silver, talc, tungsten, zinc

Business and trade: banking, health care, transportation, utilities, wholesale and retail trade

CALENDAR OF CELEBRATIONS

Whale Fest Prepare to be awed by the sheer power of the great mammals of the sea. During the spring, more than 20,000 gray whales migrate north. Daily whale-watch excursions leave from Westport.

Daffodil Festival Imagine the sight and smell of all those spring flowers. Tacoma celebrates the arrival of spring with one of the largest flower festivals in the country. Parades of floats, bands, drill teams, and mounted units keep energy running high during this three-week April event.

Puyallup Spring Fair This April celebration at the fairgrounds in Puyallup features exhibits, food, entertainment, animals, and carnival rides.

Rainfest Rain is plentiful in parts of Washington, so residents make the best of it by celebrating instead of complaining. Each April, Forks celebrates the wet weather with umbrella decorating, a bicycle rodeo, an art show, and a children's carnival.

Holland Days Enjoy a taste of Dutch heritage at this May festival in Lynden, the state's largest Dutch settlement. Learn about Dutch customs, including street scrubbing and klompen dancing, and participate in games and wooden-shoe races.

Walla Walla Balloon Stampede Each May in Walla Walla, you can watch a fleet of hot-air balloons rise slowly into the sky and sky divers jump from planes. On the ground, enjoy a barbecue and an arts and crafts show.

Ski to Sea Race Skiers, runners, canoeists, bicyclists, and sailors compete in the 85-mile relay race from Mt. Baker to Bellingham Bay in May. But you don't have to compete to get in on the fun. Bellingham welcomes the participants and fans with parades, carnival rides, games, and street fairs.

Yakima Air Fair Are you fascinated by flight? Then be sure to visit the Yakima Air Fair in June. See military, antique, warbird, and commercial aircraft. Watch fliers perform precision military aerobatics. At night, keep looking to the sky for the fireworks.

Lummi Stommish This June water carnival in Bellingham features canoe races, arts and crafts, salmon bakes, and Native American dancing.

Loggerodeo If it's July, it's time for the town of Sedro-Woolley to celebrate its logging heritage with tree-felling, climbing, and other logging competitions.

Toppenish Indian Powwow At this July festival of Indian culture in Toppenish, you can eat authentic Yakama foods, watch traditional dances and games, and enjoy a carnival, a rodeo, and a parade.

Pacific Northwest Highland Games Traditional Scottish dancers and pipe bands compete in this annual July event in Enumclaw. Food and games add to the fun.

Omak Stampede and World Famous Suicide Race In August on the Colville Indian Reservation, you can thrill to a rodeo and the famous "suicide" ride on horseback down a cliff and across the Okanogan River.

International Kite Festival On Long Beach Peninsula each August, you can observe all different kinds of kite events, from handcrafted kites to

International Kite Festival

stunt kites to lighted night flying. You can also get some pointers on flying your own kite and enjoy a fireworks display.

Makah Days This August festival in Neah Bay marks the day in 1913 when the American flag first flew over the Makah Reservation. The celebration includes an arts and crafts fair, canoe races, games, dancing, a parade, fireworks, and a salmon bake.

Harbor Days Festival As the summer winds down on Labor Day weekend, Olympia is the site of a parade, vintage tugboat races, and other entertainment.

Wooden Boat Festival Wooden boatbuilding and restoration may be a dying art, but you won't think so if you come to this October festival in Port Townsend. You will see how the boats have changed over the years as hundreds of classic wooden boats come to port.

Christmas Lighting Festival Get into the holiday spirit with the lights and decorations in Leavenworth, which is modeled after a Bavarian village. You'll also want to bundle up for an old-fashioned sleigh ride.

Yule Fest Poulsbo celebrates its Norwegian heritage with traditional foods, folk dances, games, and other celebrations of the Christmas season, including Santa's arrival by boat.

STATE STARS

William Edward Boeing (1881–1956), born in Detroit, was a pioneer in the aerospace industry. After studying at Yale University, he joined his father's lumber business in Seattle. In 1916, he founded the Pacific

Aero Products Company, which became the Boeing Airplane Company, the world's largest airplane manufacturers. In 1927, he also founded Boeing Air Transport, which later became United Airlines.

Boeing (at right)

Robert William (Bobby) Brown (1924–   ), born in Seattle, was both a baseball player and a cardiologist. He played third base for the New York Yankees and competed in four World Series in the late 1940s and early 1950s. He was also president of the American League from 1984 to 1994.

JoAnne Gunderson Carner (1939–   ), a professional golfer, was born in Kirkland. Carner was the U.S. Women's Amateur champion five times before turning professional in 1970. One of the leading money winners of the Ladies' Professional Golf Association (LPGA), she won more than 40 tournaments and was named LPGA Player of the Year three times.

JoAnne Gunderson Carner

Carol Channing (1923–   ), an actress and singer, was born in Seattle. She is best known for her musical roles on Broadway. Channing won a 1964 Tony Award for her starring role in *Hello Dolly!*, a role she has performed more than 4,500 times on Broadway as well as all over the world.

Bing Crosby (1904–1977) was a popular singer and actor from the 1930s until his death. He made more than 1,000 recordings, including the best-selling "White Christmas." In 1944, he won the best actor Academy Award for the movie *Going My Way*. Crosby was born in Tacoma.

Bing Crosby

Merce Cunningham (1919–   ) has choreographed pieces for his own dance company and for many other modern and classical dance companies around the world. He is known for his innovative techniques and has won numerous awards, including the National Medal of Arts in 1990. Cunningham was born in Centralia, began dancing at a young age, and received additional formal dance training in Seattle.

William O. Douglas (1898–1980) was a Supreme Court justice from 1939 to 1975. He was born in Minnesota and grew up in Washington. He is best remembered for his support of civil rights, conservation, and civil liberties and for his opposition to press censorship. His writings include *A Wilderness Bill of Rights* and *Of Men and Mountains*.

Tom Foley (1929–   ), who was born in Spokane, served as Speaker of the House of Representatives from 1989 to 1994. He was first elected as a Democrat to Congress in 1964. He was known for his ability to get House members to work together.

Tom Foley

Bill Gates (1955–   ), a leader in the computer industry, is one of the richest and most influential people in the world. With a friend, Paul Allen, he founded Microsoft, the first microcomputer software company. His company developed the Windows operating system, which is used in most personal computers. In the 1990s, his company also entered the online services market. Gates was born in Seattle.

Jimi Hendrix (1942–1970), a rock guitarist, singer, and composer, was born in Seattle. Combining rock and blues with a powerful guitar style, he became a legendary performer. Onstage, he was wild and intense and one of rock's best guitarists. His songs include "Purple Haze" and "Fire."

Henry "Scoop" Jackson (1912–1983), born in Everett, was a Democratic senator from Washington for 30 years beginning in 1953. In 1972 and 1976, he

Henry "Scoop" Jackson

campaigned unsuccessfully for the Democratic nomination for president. He was a liberal in social matters, supporting civil rights and the environment. However, he was more conservative in foreign affairs and supported a strong national defense.

Robert Joffrey (1930–1988) was a modern dance choreographer and founder of the Joffrey Ballet. He served as artistic director of this New York City dance company until his death. The company is known for its wide range of dance styles. Joffrey was born in Seattle.

Chief Joseph (1840–1904) was chief of the Nez Percé nation, which once occupied much of the region where Washington, Oregon, and Idaho meet. When war broke out between U.S. settlers and the Nez Percé in 1877, Chief Joseph defeated the larger U.S. forces in several battles before leading his people over rough terrain toward Canada. Federal troops overcame him 40 miles from the border. Because his people were starving and most of his warriors dead or wounded, he surrendered with the words, "I will fight no more forever." He died on the Colville Indian Reservation in Washington.

Gary Larson (1950–   ), cartoonist, was born in Tacoma. His comic strip, "The Far Side," which features visual puns and talking animals, has been one of the most popular cartoons of recent decades.

Mary McCarthy (1912–1989) was a novelist and short story writer. Her most famous work is *The Group*, a novel that follows the lives of eight graduates of Vassar College, which McCarthy attended. McCarthy was well-known for satirizing marriage and the role of women in America. She also wrote political and travel essays, book reviews, and theater criticism. McCarthy was born in Seattle.

Mary McCarthy

John McLoughlin (1784–1857) was born in Quebec and briefly studied
medicine before he joined the Hudson's Bay Company and traveled
to the Pacific Northwest. He built Fort Vancouver, now Vancouver,
Washington. His friendly policies toward American settlers angered his
Hudson's Bay bosses.

Edward R. Murrow (1908–1965) was a pioneer in radio and television
journalism. Born in North Carolina, he graduated from Washington State
College. His popular *Hear It Now* CBS radio show became a television
show, *See It Now*, which he hosted from 1951 to 1958. His most famous
show aired in March 1954, when he
attacked Senator Joseph McCarthy's
communist witch-hunt. Murrow's *Person to Person* show aired from 1953 to
1960. After leaving CBS, he headed
the United States Information Agency.

Edward R. Murrow

Theodore Roethke (1908–1963), a distinguished poet, taught at the University of Washington from 1947 to 1963. He won a Pulitzer Prize in poetry for *The Waking* and the National Book Award for the collection *Words for the Wind*. He was known for his poetic exploration into human psychology.

Smohalla (1815–1907), a member of the Wanapum Indians of the Columbia River valley, was a teacher and prophet. His Dreamer Cult dancers urged Indians to return to traditional ways of life. He claimed that through visions and dance they could restore the land to the Indians and bring back traditional lifeways. He greatly influenced the Indian efforts to resist white settlement of the region.

George Vancouver (1757–1798) was an English navigator and explorer who surveyed the west coast of North America. Between 1792 and 1794, he explored Puget Sound. He was the first explorer to survey Vancouver Island, which was named for him.

Marcus Whitman (1802–1847), a doctor and missionary, was born in Rushville, New York. He and his wife, Narcissa, founded a mission among the Cayuse Indians at Waiilatpu, near present-day Walla Walla, that became an important stopping place for settlers. The Cayuse turned on Whitman when they thought he was practicing sorcery, because he was immune to the diseases brought by the white man that were threatening the Cayuse. He and 12 others were killed by the Cayuse.

Minoru Yamasaki (1912–1986), born in Seattle, was a noted architect. His huge, dramatic buildings with Gothic arches and windows include the St. Louis, Missouri, airport, the building housing the Woodrow Wilson School of Foreign Affairs in Princeton, New Jersey, and the World Trade Center in New York City.

TOUR THE STATE

Aberdeen Museum of History (Aberdeen) This museum uses period furnishings to re-create living conditions from the town's pioneer days in the 1880s. You can tour a home, a general store, a one-room school, a blacksmith shop, and a church. Among the museum's highlights is its collection of antique fire-fighting equipment.

Grays Harbor Historical Seaport (Aberdeen) This museum and interpretive center feature exhibits on the history of maritime exploration in the Pacific Northwest, including a replica of Robert Gray's ship, on which he sailed along the Northwest coast.

Fairhaven District (Bellingham) Planners for this area, built in the late 1800s, hoped that it would become a center of commerce, the Chicago of the Northwest. Today, the historic buildings house restaurants and theaters. Take a walking tour and appreciate the past.

Bremerton Naval Museum (Bremerton) You'll receive a quick lesson in naval history by visiting this museum's displays of ship models, naval weapons and equipment, and photographs. Take a look at one of the world's oldest guns, a wooden device from China. You can also tour a naval graveyard, which has retired submarines, cruisers, and the battleship *Missouri*.

Turnbull National Wildlife Refuge (Cheney) This refuge is home to more than 200 species of birds, along with deer, elk, coyotes, beavers, mink, and other small animals. It's a great place to enjoy a hike or picnic.

Keller Historical Park (Colville) Step into the early 20th century as you tour Colville's first schoolhouse, a farmstead cabin, a trapper's cabin, a sawmill, and a building with antique farming tools. A lookout tower and museum are also part of this park.

Grand Coulee Dam (Coulee Dam) This is one of the world's largest concrete structures, and its power plants contain some of the world's largest hydro-generators. You can tour the dam, ride down to a power plant in a glass elevator, or enjoy a laser show during the summer.

Grand Coulee Dam

Fort Spokane (Coulee Dam) This was one of the last 19th-century military outposts built to maintain peace between settlers and Native Americans. Today, 4 of its 45 buildings remain, including the brick guardhouse that is now a visitors center and museum.

Olmstead Place State Park (Ellensburg) This turn-of-the-century farm has been converted into a living historical farm. It features eight buildings, wildlife, flowers and trees, and an interpretive trail. During the second weekend of September, a threshing bee and antique equipment show are held. You can also watch demonstrations of blacksmithing and plowing.

Mud Mountain Dam (Enumclaw) Bring a picnic, cool off in a wading pool, or hike the nature trails near one of the world's highest earth- and rock-fill dams.

Grant County Pioneer Village and Museum (Ephrata) Visit a pioneer homestead and village with 20 buildings, including a church, schoolhouse, saloon, barbershop, jail, and firehouse. Displays feature Native American artifacts and trace the region's natural history and early development by white settlers.

Hoquiam's "Castle" (Hoquiam) Lumber tycoon Robert Lytle built this 20-room mansion in 1897, and it still contains Victorian furnishings. A saloon has been re-created to give you a feel for the period.

Mount Rainier National Park (Packwood) Hike, fish, ski, mountain climb, picnic, camp, and explore nature at this spectacular park, which is home to mountain goats, mountain lions, bears, elk, and eagles. Mount Rainier, 14,410 feet above sea level, is the fifth-highest mountain in the lower 48 states and the largest volcano in the Cascade Range.

Mount St. Helens Visitors Center (Castle Rock) This site includes a walk-through model of the Mount St. Helens volcano, which last erupted in 1980. It also features a history of the mountain, volcano-monitoring equipment, views of the volcano, and a nature trail. Some hiking trails cut through nearby Mount St. Helens National Volcanic Monument, which covers 110,000 acres of forestland that is renewing itself after being destroyed by the eruption. Helicopter and airplane sight-seeing tours are also available from area airports.

Makah Cultural and Research Center (Neah Bay) At this museum, you can learn about Northwest Indian culture. The center includes exhibits on

Makah and other Northwest Coast Indians, 500-year-old artifacts, a 2,000-year-old Makah village, canoes, and a longhouse.

State Capitol Group (Olympia) On the grounds of this complex are beautiful Japanese cherry trees, a replica of Copenhagen's Tivoli Gardens' fountain, sunken gardens, and World War I and Vietnam memorials. The 287-foot capitol dome is one of the largest in the world.

Olympic National Park (Port Angeles) This park features a wide range of terrain, including seashores and snowcapped mountains, glaciers and rain forests. The park's rain forests are among the wettest places in the nation, receiving 135 inches of rain annually. Visitors can camp, fish, hike, or cruise on paddle-wheel boats.

Pike Place Market (Seattle) This vibrant market is the oldest continuously operating farmers' market in the United States, selling goods ranging from vegetables to antiques. It opened in 1907, and many of the original buildings have been restored.

Seattle Center (Seattle) You'll find a lot to do within this site of the 1962 world's fair. The grounds include gardens, plazas, sculptures, and fountains. Both the children's museum and the Pacific Science Center include many hands-on exhibits. Ride to the top of the 605-foot Space Needle and look out over the Puget Sound region and then spend some time at the Fun Forest Amusement Park.

The Seattle Aquarium (Seattle) This watery exhibit features a 400,000-gallon underwater viewing center of Northwest marine life. The tide pool exhibit re-creates the state's coast, and marine mammals such as sea otters and seals swim in pools.

Boeing Field—King County International Airport (Seattle) Forty aircraft are on display at this museum of flight. Exhibits include a restored World War II Corsair, a 1929 Boeing Model 80A-1, an Apollo command module, and other recent jets.

Point Defiance Zoo and Aquarium (Tacoma) At this zoo, you'll get to know the animals of the Pacific Rim, including polar bears, beluga whales, sharks, sea otters, and walruses. Habitats featured include Arctic tundra, Puget Sound's rocky shores, and the tropics of the South Pacific. The North Pacific Aquarium displays the marine life of Puget Sound. The Discovery Reef Aquarium is teeming with tropical fish and sharks.

Fort Vancouver National Historic Site (Vancouver) In 1849, the first U.S. military outpost in the Northwest was founded in Vancouver. It was closed in 1860 but has been partially reconstructed and now includes a kitchen, a washhouse, a stockade wall, a bakehouse, a blacksmith shop, and other facilities.

FUN FACTS

In 1870, two climbers reached the summit of Mount Rainier and planted United States flags. This was the first recorded climb to the summit by white explorers. Neither of the flags they planted, however, had the 37 stars appropriate for the time. One bore only 13 stars because it had to be sewn in a hurry the night before the expedition. The other was 11 years old and had only 32 stars.

In the early 20th century, loggers strapped 1,000-foot-long bundles of logs together with 150 tons of chain to form rafts. They floated these giant rafts from the Columbia River to San Diego.

The first city monorail service in the country began operation in Seattle in 1962. It connected downtown Seattle with the world's fair grounds.

FIND OUT MORE

Want to learn more about Washington? Check your local library or bookstore for these titles:

GENERAL STATE BOOKS

Breakstone, Steve. *Washington Walkabout*. Port Angeles, WA: Balance Books, 1997.

Fradin, Dennis B., and Judith Bloom. *Washington*. Chicago: Children's Press, 1994.

Powell, E. S. *Washington*. Minneapolis: Lerner Publications, 1993.

BOOKS ABOUT PLACES AND PEOPLE

Baskas, Harriet, and Adam Woog. *Atomic Marbles and Branding Irons: A Guide to Museums, Collections, and Roadside Curiosities in Washington and Oregon*. Seattle: Sasquatch Books, 1993.

Bergman, Donna. *Kids Go! Seattle*. Santa Fe: John Muir Publications, 1996.

Brewster, David, and David M. Buerge. *Washingtonians: A Biographical Portrait of the State*. Seattle: Sasquatch Books, 1988.

Cone, Molly. *Come Back, Salmon: How a Group of Dedicated Kids Adopted Pigeon Creek and Brought It Back to Life.* San Francisco: Sierra Club Books for Children, 1992.

George, Jean Craighead. *The Moon of the Mountain Lions.* New York: Harper-Collins, 1991.

Greene, Frank L. *Hall of Honor: A Gallery of One Hundred Eminent Washingtonians.* Seattle: Washington State Historical Society, 1989.

Hirschi, Ron. *People of Salmon and Cedar.* New York: Cobblehill Books, 1996.

Sharpe, Susan. *Spirit Quest.* New York: Bradbury Books, 1991.

Snelson, Karin. *Seattle.* New York: Dillon Press, 1992.

VIDEOS

Destination Seattle. Seattle: Wehman Videos, 1996.

Over Washington. New York: Ambrose Video, 1989.

Seattle Chronicle. Seattle: Wehman Video, 1992.

Washington's Parks and Forests. Portland, OR: Encounter Video, 1990.

Washington State: A Scenic Tour. Seattle: Hatzoff Productions, 1996.

Washington State's Cascade Loop. Seattle: Hatzoff Productions, 1993.

Washington State's Olympic Peninsula. Seattle: Hatzoff Productions, 1995.

Washington State's San Juan Islands. Seattle: Hatzoff Productions, 1994.

CD-ROMS

Mount Rainier: Where the River Begins. Nederland, CO: Rocky Mountain Digital Press.

Oregon Trail II. Minneapolis: MECC, 1995.

U.S. Geography: The West. Dallas: ZCI Publishing, 1994.

WEBSITES

Home Page Washington: www.state.wa.us/

Washington State Tourism Home Page: www.tourism.wa.gov/

INDEX

Chart, graph, and illustration page numbers are in boldface.